The
Constitutional
Logic of
Affirmative
Action

The Constitutional Logic of Affirmative Action

by RONALD J. FISCUS

edited by Stephen L. Wasby

DUKE UNIVERSITY PRESS

Durham and London 1992

.

© 1992 Duke University Press
All rights reserved
Printed in the United States of America
on acid-free paper ∞
Library of Congress Cataloging-in-Publication Data
appear on the last printed page of this book.

This book is dedicated
to the students of Skidmore College,
to whom Ron Fiscus devoted his life
as a teacher and friend
and
to the hope for increased
fairness, reason, and justice
for which he strove.

contents

editor's preface

This is a book on affirmative action. It is a provocative book that demands that the reader enter into the author's framework and follow a well-developed argument. This is also a book that, because of the controversy surrounding affirmative action and the rhetoric that has come to envelop that subject, asks the reader to suspend prejudices, preconceptions, and judgment until the reader has followed the argument through its development. (We return to this need to suspend judgment below, in A Call to the Reader.) The controversy surrounding affirmative action and the rhetoric that has come to envelop that subject have engendered a clear need for increased precision in thinking and talking about affirmative action programs, recognized not only by observers but also by some firm supporters of such programs.[1] This volume makes such a contribution. As affirmative action will, in one variant or another, be on the public agenda for some time, the author's powerful and elegant argument needs to be attended to carefully—and heeded.

Before proceeding, we need to "get back to basics" with respect to affirmative action. Rhetoric to the contrary notwithstanding, *affirmative action* does NOT—repeat NOT—equal *quotas*. An affirmative action plan *may* include quotas, but *need not* do so. *Affirmative action* is a term encompassing a range of actions that go beyond compensation to individuals for direct individual injury. The concept subsumes a set of programs ranging from, at its mildest, wide advertising of positions to prompt more people to apply or extensive recruitment of potential applicants, through the use of ranges and goals in hiring, to, ultimately, at its most severe, the use of fixed quotas for hiring and promotion. We must remember that even this use has been approved by the courts after judicial findings of purposeful systemic discrimination. Yet despite the range of mechanisms just noted, many opponents of affirmative action label *all* disliked programs "quotas" because of the negative resonance of that term, as in the current debate over proposed civil rights legislation (see Epilogue, pp. 119–23).

The Author's Argument

Starting from the presumption that the Supreme Court, in its affirmative action cases, needs a firmer theoretical understanding of the rights both of individuals and of groups, Ronald Fiscus develops a central argument through a combination of constitutional law and political theory. The argument is that proportionate quotas are justified in terms of distributive justice. The author has set out not only to analyze and to evaluate pronouncements by the Supreme Court and some contemporary political philosophers but also to stake out a position. He is not simply engaging in analysis of court cases for its own sake; he not only criticizes but brings the cases to bear on his position.

The author develops his argument by stipulating equality at birth and by working from an assumption of no race-related differences in intellectual ability at birth, that is, absolute equality, with a further stipulation of a nonracist society, so that how race and other factors affect the initial distribution can be examined. Fiscus, an idealist, is asking, "Let us assume a society without racism; departures from the initial racial proportions in that society can only be attributed to racism; how would we go about fixing them?"

The author's view is that most affirmative action programs, even with quotas, advance race-related claims of distributive justice and generally are the only way to advance such claims—and can do so both for disadvantaged minorities and advantaged nonminorities. He argues for quotas but advocates a particular type of quota—one limited to the posited population ratio—and devotes much of his argument to explaining this concept.

In his argument the author deals with the principal criticism of affirmative action programs, that they are unfair to white males (the "innocent persons" argument), which supporters of affirmative action have failed to rebut adequately. His view is that properly conceived affirmative action programs do not discriminate against nonminority individuals. Affirmative action, the author argues, is not violative of the rights of white individuals when it guarantees minorities the proportion of society's goods they would have had in a nonracist environment. He argues against quotas that exceed the minority proportion of the population—that is, disproportionate quotas.

In taking his position, the author has adopted what might be called a group perspective on the law rather than restricting himself to what might be called the individual perspective. Alan Freeman has spoken of the perpetrator perspective in racial discrimination cases—a perspective like the individual perspective—in which one cannot have remedies for racial discrimination unless an identifiable individual has committed a fault-based act on another individual.[2] In contrast, in the victim perspective, one examines group characteristics and allows remedies reaching beyond the "identifiable discriminated-against individual" by taking the victimized group into account; affirmative action programs partake of, even if they do not consciously adopt, the latter perspective.

The principal focus of the argument is on the Supreme Court's affirmative action rulings, from the Bakke* case of 1976 on quotas in admission to medical school through the Croson case thirteen years later on the Richmond, Virginia "minority business set-aside" program. The author explains and analyzes the Court's cases extensively and applies his central argument to them. Along with the Court's opinions, the author uses commentary on those rules and the scholarly literature on affirmative action to develop his argument. (Developments subsequent to the conclusion of the manuscript are discussed in an epilogue provided by the editor.)

The focus of the author's argument is on affirmative action programs relating to race, primarily with respect to African Americans. The framework is, however, far more broadly applicable. The au-

---

*See the Table of Cases for citations to cases and references to pages of this volume on which they are discussed.

thor has not provided a separate discussion with respect to affirmative action programs related to gender discrimination; however, his argument is also applicable to those programs. The Supreme Court has treated race and gender differently for some purposes. Racial distinctions receive "strict scrutiny" while distinctions based on gender receive a lower (intermediate) level of scrutiny. Yet the Court has generally treated challenges to affirmative action plans as "all of a piece," regardless of whether race or sex is involved, and has certainly done so under Title VII of the Civil Rights Act of 1964, which outlaws job discrimination based on race or sex. We can see this identity of treatment in the discussion of *Johnson v. Santa Clara County*, in which the Court upheld the promotion of a woman when her employer had specifically taken gender into account. That ruling certainly is consonant with the language in Justice Powell's prevailing opinion in the *Bakke* case that race may permissibly be considered in deciding admissions to colleges and universities. Thus, in considering affirmative action cases, race and gender can reasonably be considered together.

The author's focus on affirmative action programs, and most particularly on quotas, means that most of his attention has been given to employment discrimination. The Supreme Court's first two affirmative action cases involved higher education: *DeFunis v. Odegaard*, in which the Court ruled the dispute moot because, by the time of its decision, the complainant was about to graduate from the law school from which he had allegedly been improperly excluded because of its affirmative action plan, and *Bakke*, the initial and perhaps quintessential affirmative action case. Thereafter, the Court's affirmative action rulings involved employment, the area with which we most closely associate the concept of affirmative action; however, its 1990 *Metro Broadcasting* decision (see Epilogue) involved ownership of television stations.

Despite this focus on employment, the issues raised by affirmative action and quotas pervade all areas of policy involving racial discrimination. Thus we find them when we consider voting rights. This can be seen most clearly in *United Jewish Organizations v. Carey* (1976). In this case the question was whether, under the Voting Rights Act of 1965, the attorney general could insist that the population of a legislative district be at least 65 percent black to facilitate the election by minorities of someone they felt directly represented them, where in so doing a community of whites (Hasidic Jews) was split between districts. The Court upheld the attorney general's action under the statute, but several justices spoke in terms resonating with the same concerns later expressed more explicitly in *Bakke* and subsequent affirmative action cases.

Questions concerning voting rights also touch on the "innocent victim" issue. As the Court, in its voting rights cases, turned from the Voting Rights Act's initial concern—exclusion of minorities from the right to vote—to "vote dilution" (the diminished opportunity of a racial group to elect a representative from its own ranks), concerns about "proportional representation" and disadvantage to whites increased. As Bruce Cain has observed, "The most common objection to the recent evolution in voting rights is that it bestows special representational advantages upon some racial and ethnic groups but not others and pulls the U.S. back away from its much-cherished ideal of a color-blind society."[3] Indeed, there may well be a linkage between voting rights and affirmative action programs, as usually more narrowly conceptualized as applying to education and particularly to employment: "The backlash against the implementation of the Voting Rights Act must be seen in the context of similar backlash against set-aside programs, remedial preferential hiring or admissions policies for nonwhites, and the like. Resentments toward affirmative action in other realms inevitability spill over into voting rights issues."[4]

Comparable issues also arise in connection with school desegregation. Speaking of what he called the "corrective theory of school desegregation," in which desegregative actions are taken to correct past violations, James Liebman suggested that the redistributive effects of such actions are unsatisfactory to both whites and blacks. They are too corrective from whites' perspective, "by imposing remedial burdens on parents and children who, for all corrective theory can show, are 'innocent,' and by conferring remedial benefits on at least some black children who, according to the corrective theory are not victims."[5] At the same time, desegregation is insufficiently corrective from the perspective of African Americans "because it fails to compensate actual black victims of intentional discrimination for the vast majority of the injuries segregation causes them, not the least of which is a lifetime of lost or decreased earnings of the sort that the desegregation cases have never deemed compensable."[6] It is for this reason that Liebman, who strongly supports desegregation, argued instead for what he called "reformative theory" (see Epilogue).

A call to the reader. Because of the heightened emotion stimulated by the words "affirmative action," the reader is invited—indeed, encouraged—to enter into the author's framework and is asked to suspend judgment. The reader should keep in mind that the author is making a philosophical argument based on certain clearly stated working assumptions, not conducting an empirical study. This is not hypothesis-driven social science research but, as its title suggests, an examination of the logic of arguments—the author's, contemporary theorists', and those of Supreme Court justices. One should therefore resist the temptation to quarrel with the particular racial ratio the author chooses and should remember that economists regularly, and fruitfully, work from such assumptions.

The author was stimulated to grapple with one of the century's major public policy issues by the quality of logic (or lack thereof) underlying the pronouncements of that major policy actor, the Supreme Court, and particularly by the majority's reliance on the "innocent victims" argument. In focusing on the logic of the basic aspects of central policy issues, he did not, however, set for himself the task of developing detailed proposals. For example, he did not develop detailed consideration of how to deal with the racial ratios he stipulated when those ratios change over generations as a result of "intermixture." For the reader, the answer—for now, at least—should be that such changes can be accommodated because the particular ratio is not fixed. Likewise, he did not work on the question of how to define a victimized racial group, with matters such as whether children from racially mixed marriages should be considered minorities or whether recent immigrants from, say, Africa or the Caribbean should be included among those who would receive the fruits of the distributive justice of which he writes in this volume. The answer here, too, is that those developing or implementing the programs have not found it insuperably difficult to provide the definitions and stipulations necessary for program implementation, just as those who enforced segregation found it possible to define who was a Negro in terms of the percentage of "Negro blood" a person carried, as the state of Louisiana did in a statute until only a couple of decades ago.

In what may be a more difficult step, the reader is also asked to separate evaluation of the argument from the disagreement many undoubtedly will experience, in whole or in part. One must remember that philosophical arguments should not be rejected simply because of an individual's animosities or because they seem out of step with public opinion. The author's proposal will displease not only those opposed to quotas in any form, but is also likely to displease those who would implement quotas that seek to provide a speedy remedy for underrepresentation of racial minorities and women in the workplace or university student body by applying disproportionate quotas until a certain goal is reached. Present rhetoric surrounding the topic of affirmative action will make the requested suspension of judgment difficult. That rhetoric, which makes it possible for many people to attack *all* affirmative action plans under the guise of disagreeing with hated "quotas," also makes it possible for the socially advantaged to avoid coming to grips with racism and sexism, whether it is subtle or institutional or takes the form of outright discrimination against racial minorities or women.

The book's history. The author of this book, Ronald J. Fiscus, died on 18 May 1990, just short of his forty-second birthday, after serving on the faculty of Skidmore College for ten years. In addition to his considerable effect on his Skidmore students and on colleagues there and elsewhere, he left behind, along with the rough outline and some building blocks of what was to have been his next project,[7] the complete and already highly polished manuscript that has become this book.

Somewhat from the sidelines, I had seen this book grow and develop, as Ron presented an earlier version to the New York State Political Science Association (where it won the prize for best paper) and then a longer version to a graduate seminar at the State University of New York at Albany. I thought both versions, and particularly the more highly developed and much-extended version presented to the graduate seminar, consummate work combining constitutional law and political theory and effectively informed by a vision, and thus it was a pleasure to play some small part in providing finishing touches. The manuscript, an editor's dream, needed little work prior to submission for publication. Beyond completing documentation for some footnotes, I have only moved some interesting thoughts from extended endnotes to the body of the text and redistributed one chapter's several segments of constitutional argument to places where they seemed better to assist the flow of the author's argument.

Acknowledgments. In preparation of the manuscript and all the other tasks surrounding this enterprise I have had unstinting assistance from several key people. Erwin Levine, professor of government at Skidmore College and at one time Ron Fiscus's department chair, was always available to respond to my thinking and to provide advice; his assistance with the editing was invaluable. Chris Glenn greatly facilitated the production of a "clean" manuscript by translating the editor's requests into keyboard commands. For all of us, and particularly for them because of their close association with Ron, to assist in bringing into the world the labor of love of one who, because of his untimely death, was unable to see it come into the full light of day, has itself been a labor of love. They and I also thank Mary Ellen Fischer and Susan Daly for providing important moral support.

Especial thanks go to Larry Malley of the Duke University Press, who never met Ron, for making the publication of the manuscript possible, and for his thoughtfulness and understanding. This is not the first time Larry has facilitated a valuable addition to the corpus of law-related literature by a scholar who most unfortunately died at an early age,[8] and for that the scholarly profession and all those who read this book are in his debt.

Stephen L. Wasby
Albany, New York
June 1991

author's preface

[Editor's Note: Ronald Fiscus completed only a few pages of what he intended to be the concluding chapter of this book. It seems fitting to use as the Author's Preface the brief statement below, the beginning of that unfinished segment. It stands by itself as an effective statement of the author's credo.]

Life has always been unfair. It is unfair now. And it will always be unfair. People have treated people unfairly through the ages, whether the mechanism has been social class and economic inequality, ethnic or racial or gender-based prejudice, physical appearance, xenophobia, simple thoughtlessness or meanness of spirit, or any of a host of other factors that people have mistakenly believed were valid indicators of how other people should be treated.

Beyond that, life itself, or nature, is unfair. Natural disasters hit hard and unevenly, and often without regard for personal blame or credit. Flood and drought and famine, earthquake, hurricane, disease (including those whose causes are unknown and those at least partially hereditary or environmentally induced), the proverbial bolt of lightning, and innumerable other genuine accidents and "acts of God"—these horrendous punishments rarely, if ever, seem merited by any ascertainable individual crimes.

The progress of law—when it has been true progress—has been the result of its ability to reflect the growing rationality that modern societies are capable of. It has been said that the law despises irrationality, and indeed the traditional concept of due process of law is at least loosely tied to the idea that every law must have some plausible reason. This explains why the law can help—and has often helped—diminish some kinds of unfairness but cannot help diminish others.

Unfairness is usually a form of not playing by the rules. One of the most basic rules of civilized societies, often underappreciated and usually unspoken, is that people should be judged and treated according to criteria that are relevant to their true merit. That is, they should be free of prejudgments that are needlessly general or false or exaggerated. To the greatest extent possible, people should be judged according to their actual, individual characteristics—and not by characteristics irrelevant to the thing in question. To do otherwise is to act irrationally, to treat people as if they had certain characteristics when they do not, or to assume that they are un-suited for consideration when they may be well suited. Behavior engendered by prejudice wastes human potential, frustrates legiti-mate hopes, and perpetuates misunderstanding and hatred. And, of course, behavior so engendered is behavior engendered by a lie.

The law can and often does reflect these sentiments. One thing is clear: even if we were to succeed in eliminating completely the effects of racial consciousness, we would hardly have achieved a perfect society. There would doubtless remain many and varied kinds of injustices.

In any case, one may concede that life is and will continue to be unfair without undermining in the slightest the assumption that diminishing unfairness is a basic task of law and society. What can reasonably be done must be done, for how can we ever hope to attain the just society if we accept injustices along the way?

Ronald J. Fiscus

The
Constitutional
Logic of
Affirmative
Action

introduction

In a lengthy dissent in 1974 William O. Douglas was the first
Supreme Court justice to engage in an extensive discussion of
affirmative action. Four years later, in the *Bakke* case,[1] a seriously
divided Supreme Court issued its first pronouncement on the controversial subject. After a hiatus of several years the Court handed
down a major decision in 1984, three more in 1986, and two more
in 1987.[2] Each of those decisions received considerable attention
from news media and Court scholars, in part because they were
perceived as rebuffs to the Reagan administration, which had maintained a highly visible opposition to most forms of affirmative
action—more specifically, to quotas. In each of the cases the administration had opposed affirmative action either as plaintiff or as
amicus curiae, and more than a few observers were surprised at the
extent to which the Court resisted the administration's pressure
and on the whole affirmed its commitment to affirmative action—
in some ways even strengthening it.

But the Court was still not finished. Many of the new decisions
had been decided by the narrowest of margins. Just as he had in so
many other areas, Justice Lewis Powell had supplied the critical fifth
vote in three of the four most controversial and difficult cases.[3] In
four of the six cases he had voted to uphold affirmative action.
When Justice Powell announced his retirement in 1987, it gave the
Reagan administration one more chance to change the direction of

the Court, and many observers wondered if the law on affirmative action would prove unstable. It did.

In 1989, with Justice Anthony Kennedy providing the crucial fifth vote, the Supreme Court handed down two more major affirmative action decisions.[4] In one of them, *City of Richmond v. J. A. Croson Company*,[5] the Court struck down an ordinance that channeled 30 percent of city construction money to minority-owned contracting firms. But apart from reaching a result hostile to affirmative action, the decision was noteworthy for its insistence that affirmative action plans may only be justified by particularized, identifiable past discrimination *by the group or institution to be remediated*. Previously, it had been uncertain whether a general racial proportionality might be used as a benchmark and/or justification for affirmative action quotas in particular cases. The *Richmond* case signaled, more unambiguously than any earlier case had, the Court's antipathy to general racial proportionality, either as a benchmark or as a justification for any given affirmative action plan.

The *Richmond* decision was probably inevitable, not so much because of the slimness of the earlier support for affirmative action as because of its theoretical shakiness. In a decade of struggle with the issue, the Court never accepted the argument that racial disparity was in and of itself evidence of discrimination that would justify affirmative action quotas. That, of course, would have made the issue simple. But apart from other problems with that sweeping justification, the argument always came up against the justices' belief—sometimes explicitly stated, sometimes assumed *sub silentio*—that affirmative action plans virtually always disadvantage white (or male) individuals who are themselves innocent of discriminatory behavior. Before 1989, then, the Court was caught in the untenable position of acknowledging that affirmative action often (or always) violated individual rights, while nonetheless holding that society's compelling interest in general racial (or sexual) fairness sometimes transcended those rights.

That line of reasoning relied less on constitutional principles than on human judgments about what kind of a society we ought to be, and as such it could be persuasive only to justices sympathetic to the goals of affirmative action. Under the circumstances, it is not surprising that replacing a moderately conservative justice with an apparently more conservative justice would result in the Court reaching different conclusions about affirmative action.

What the Court needed then, and what it continues to need, is a firmer theoretical understanding of the rights of both individuals and groups in affirmative action cases. For proponents of affirmative action it is late in the day, indeed. It would have been far better to have helped set the Court on firmer ground before a majority of the Court adopted limits on affirmative action programs.

There are two principal reasons for the use in this work of the term *affirmative action* rather than *benign* or *reverse discrimination*. The first is consistency with the central argument that properly conceived affirmative action programs do not in fact discriminate against nonminority individuals. The second is that although this work centers more on racial than other forms of discrimination, *affirmative action* seems to apply far more broadly to all forms of discrimination. Such terms as *benign* or *reverse discrimination* are usually applied to specific areas of discrimination—such as gender or narrowly to race. Thus I use the term *affirmative action* throughout this work to avoid any inference that my arguments apply only to racial discrimination. Moreover, *benign discrimination* does not mean in gender cases what it means in race cases. Benign discrimination toward women may mean affirmative action—as in actively attempting to bring more women into an occupation—but it may also mean preserving for women a benefit denied to men. That sort of discrimination is not, in fact, benign at all because it is almost always based on stereotypes of appropriate sex roles or on generalizations of female dependency or vulnerability or inferiority and because the perpetuation of such preferences tends to "keep women in their place"; thus the Court has properly viewed it with suspicion since the early 1970s.

The issue of affirmative action is older than the current national debates.[6] By now, however, it would seem that every possible argument—both for it and against it—should have been aired in the law journals or in the journals of philosophy and public affairs or in the editorial pages of the nation's newspapers. One would think that everything worth saying must have been said somewhere by now. Certainly the Court's opinions must have been so thoroughly analyzed that nothing much new about them could be said.

And, indeed, the commentary has been both voluminous and generally enlightening.[7] What, one wonders, could possibly be added at this point? The truth is that one central issue in the affirmative action debate has never been well argued.

There are numerous arguments for and against affirmative action, and there are even several strands of the purely constitutional argument. Affirmative action may be justified in terms of compensation for past injustices or as a cure for the lingering effects of those injustices. Or it may be defended or attacked on grounds of utility: for lowering the level of competence in the society, or raising the level of competence in the long run as more of the society's individual potential is tapped; for polarizing the society along racial or gender lines, or promoting long-term harmony and tolerance through initially forced familiarity, and through provision of role models that will help make preferential treatment unnecessary in the future. Because of the potential for stigmatizing preferred minorities as "unable to make it on their own," affirmative action is almost as frequently said to be harmful to disadvantaged groups as it is said to be helpful.[8] Defenders of affirmative action argue that most of the initial suspicion that preferred individuals lack merit abates as soon as the individuals prove their competence, as they usually do, and that whatever suspicion remains unabated is really prejudice looking for an excuse.

But above all, affirmative action is criticized for being unfair to white males who are displaced by the programs even though they have not themselves caused particular harm to blacks or women. The charge is that such programs are always unfair to the individuals (white or male) against whom the preferential treatment is directed, unless those individuals themselves participated in the discrimination against the now-preferred minorities. If they have not personally participated in the particular discrimination in question, then they are considered innocent, and the imposition of an affirmative action quota that disadvantages them is considered an unfair act of discrimination against them simply because they are white or male. For convenience, I have called this the "innocent persons" argument.

The innocent persons argument has gained some respectability with some commentators. Alan H. Goldman recognized in his 1979 book that quotas based on race or sex "tend to violate rights of . . .

presently most qualified white males, who are not liable for past injuries." Some argue that the burdens of what they call "reverse discrimination" when visited on innocent whites are "an independent moral wrong not justifiable for reasons of policy or convenience."[9] The argument also appears to have been accepted to some degree or another by most, if not all, of the Supreme Court justices since *Bakke* was decided more than a decade ago. Judging by both earlier and recent decisions, the major difference on this matter is that some justices believe that white males are always unfairly victimized by quotas and that such victimization is never constitutionally permissible, while other justices believe that white males may be innocent but that their rights may sometimes be overridden by the transcendent justifications of affirmative action (see pp. 39–44 in this volume). Either way, the essential assertion of innocence is uncontested.

The suspicion arises that the Court's supporters of affirmative action have failed to find a way to rebut the innocent persons argument. Its acceptance, whether explicit or tacit, by both supporters and opponents means that the only difference between them is the former's willingness to sacrifice the rights of individual white males to achieve the assertedly greater end of fairness to groups. The result has been a series of decisions up to 1989 which in their aggregate supported a broad (though not complete) array of affirmative action programs yet failed to answer the nagging constitutional questions about fairness to white males harmed by those programs.[10] In place of persuasive constitutional analysis the Court majority substituted essentially policy arguments—or, in the case of Justice Powell, subjective distinctions about degrees of individual harm.

Justice Powell's "degree-of-harm" test appeared as early as 1980, in *Fullilove v. Klutznick*, where he concurred in upholding a public works set-aside provision because it posed "no excessive burden" on white contractors; the burden was simply "not so great that the set-aside must be disapproved."[11] But the fullest expression of this rationale occurred in Justice Powell's plurality opinion in the 1986 *Wygant* case, where he wrote that the rationale was based on the premise that "as part of this nation's dedication to eradicating racial discrimination, innocent persons may be called upon to bear some of the burden of the remedy."[12]

While that statement is significant for revealing Justice Powell's (and the *Wygant* plurality's) acceptance of the innocent persons argument, the most distinguishing characteristic of this affirmative action jurisprudence is that only "some of the burden" may constitutionally be placed on these "innocent persons." For these justices, affirmative action was acceptable in hiring but not in firing:

> In cases involving valid hiring goals, the burden to be borne by innocent individuals is diffused to a considerable extent among society generally. Though hiring goals may burden some innocent individuals, they simply do not impose the same kind of injury that layoffs impose. Denial of a future employment opportunity is not as intrusive as loss of an existing job.
>
> While hiring goals impose a diffuse burden, often foreclosing only one of several opportunities, layoffs impose the entire burden of achieving racial equality on particular individuals, often resulting in serious disruption of their lives. That burden is too intrusive.[13]

A year after *Wygant*, Justice Powell included promotions with hiring. In *Paradise*, he upheld a rather drastic one-for-one promotional quota for Alabama state troopers on the ground that "the effect . . . on innocent white troopers is likely to be relatively diffuse."[14] Quoting from his *Wygant* opinion, and contrasting the two cases, he argued that "unlike layoff requirements, the promotion requirement at issue in this case does not 'impose the entire burden of achieving racial equality on particular individuals,' and does not disrupt seriously the lives of innocent individuals."[15]

Whether or not it was due to Justice Powell's influence, a closely divided Court has sometimes given the appearance of relying on such a degree-of-harm test—as, for instance, in the "no unnecessary trammeling" formula of *United Steelworkers v. Weber*[16] or in Justice White's opinions.[17] But Justice Powell was never able to command a majority for the explicit view that the constitutionality of race-based policies is to be determined by how much disruption they cause to how many people.[18]

That should not be surprising. As Kathleen Sullivan has noted, the "suggestion that the social costs and benefits of affirmative action may be judicially weighed and balanced . . . invokes the spectra of social engineering" that the Court desperately wishes to avoid.[19] Moreover, "Justice Powell's distinction between hiring and layoffs may have intuitive appeal as a compromise between always taking white innocence into account and never doing so. But viewing white sacrifice as a matter of degree cannot dispel the perception of innocence that . . . makes even lesser sacrifices seem unfair."[20] That is, as long as whites are perceived as innocent, no degree of burdening will appear principled. The point can be made even more forcefully: Until the premise of innocence is effectively refuted, no degree of burdening will be principled. But in any case, Sullivan noted, the Court's judgments here are likely to be subjective and dubious. It will not be easy to convince working-class whites "that they need not pay for the sins of discrimination with jobs they already have, but that they must do so with jobs or promotions they might otherwise have gotten but for affirmative action."[21] As if to prove her right, Justice Scalia's opinion in Santa Clara County forcefully articulated the "shocking" discrimination against an individual who likely would have been promoted but for an affirmative action plan.[22]

Thus, even if one had been pleased with the results of the pre-1989 cases, one could not have been happy with the state of the law itself. Even if the Court had not changed direction with its new appointees, as it apparently has, the Court's affirmative action decisions would have continued to rest on a shaky defense. Until the innocent persons argument is squarely met, no defense of affirmative action is going to be wholly persuasive. If the argument could be rebutted, or at least narrowed to its proper application, then some critics of affirmative action might well be persuaded of its constitutionality, while others would at least be deprived of a seemingly powerful argument against it. On the other side, supporters of affirmative action would gain new confidence that their judgment is correct. It thus seems imperative to clarify the debate even at this late date. Given the Court's continuing theoretical lack, it is much too soon to consider the Richmond decision definitive.

Finally, the innocent persons argument is more than an important constitutional argument. It is a widely held, racially polarizing social argument. The near-universal belief in it is without doubt the single most powerful source of popular resentment of affirmative action. If the belief could somehow be undercut, the resentment toward affirmative action and the associated racial polarization might be diminished. Thus, whether the focus is on constitutional or on social, political, or moral arguments, the resolution of the innocent persons argument is crucial. If the perception of unfairness to white males could be changed, affirmative action would stand on firmer ground, both theoretically and practically.

Compensatory versus Distributive Justice

The rationale I offer here is one of distributive justice rather than of compensatory justice. As Kent Greenawalt has pointed out,[23] these two arguments are difficult to separate when the general rationale is the need to correct the effects of past discrimination. But the two arguments are, in fact, distinct. Properly conceived, compensatory justice is the claim to compensation for discrete and "finished" harm done to minority group members or their ancestors. To award damages for prior suffering is to engage in compensatory justice, whatever the form of the suffering. Simplified for our purposes, distributive justice as a matter of equal protection is the claim an individual or group has to the positions or advantages or benefits they would have been awarded under fair conditions—fair conditions being identified here with the absence of invidious discrimination.[24] When we consider minimum requirements of equal protection, distributive justice requires that *whatever advantages are allowed under fair conditions be allowed to everyone*, regardless of race or gender. Our definition is not intended to, and does not, preclude the attachment of limits on permissible advantages. It simply insists that whatever the limits are, they must be the same for everyone.

In making affirmative action claims, confusion arises because the language of compensatory justice is as often employed to defend distributive justice as it is employed to defend compensatory justice. That is, it is frequently argued that affirmative action programs are necessary to "compensate" minorities for the harm done to them in the past. But unless further clarification is made, it is uncertain whether the argument refers to past harms so great that their victims (or, more likely, their victims' descendants) deserve to be compensated, or to past harms that have continuing, disabling effects. If the referent is the former, the argument is indeed one of compensatory justice, but if it is the latter, the argument is essentially one of distributive justice.

Distributive justice is a claim of justice in the present; compensatory justice is a claim of retroactive justice, of justice in or for the past. In some cases, of course, the two merge, as when a past injustice is said to have continuing effects. But in that case the distributive justice argument has subsumed or incorporated the compensation claim; the argument says that in an ideal world, such harms have to be corrected—*ended*, really—even if belatedly. Claims of distributive justice are thus always centered on an abstract present; if the past is brought into the argument, it is always incorporated into the terms of the ideal distribution of goods—that is, a distribution that would be just for all persons in all times.

That affirmative action programs have been frequently justified in terms of compensatory justice[25] is highly unfortunate. Such a justification is problematical in these cases, and its vulnerabilities have been seized on by critics—including, perhaps most importantly, Supreme Court justices—to discredit affirmative action. Arguments of compensatory justice in the context of affirmative action run up against our strongly ingrained general opposition to group responsibility and group entitlement—punishing or rewarding an individual simply because he or she belongs to a group.

Group responsibility and group entitlement are appropriate when the characteristic defining the group is of primary relevance to the reward or punishment in question, and when the group behavior can be said to be the product of voluntary effort by the individuals who comprise it—as in teams or conspiracies of all kinds. But it is not appropriate, we generally believe, when individuals are defined and treated as part of a group whose behavior they do not necessarily endorse or have significant control over. It is especially inappropriate when the individuals are not free to withdraw from the group—as is the case when the group is defined by race.

More specifically, there are two related objections to the compensatory justice argument for affirmative action. They are grounded in the complementary principles that compensation should be paid to the one harmed and that it should be paid by the one who caused the harm. Affirmative action programs based on compensatory justice may fail the first principle in several ways, most obviously because of generational and socioeconomic class differences. While perhaps no one would go so far as to assert that there is no continuing harm to racial minorities in the current generation, few would dispute that the most egregious harm occurred in past generations, and in any case that is the harm most typically asserted as justification for reverse discrimination now. To hold that descendants of the millions of blacks harmed throughout our history are entitled to compensation for the long-past injury of their ancestors is to violate the first principle of compensatory justice, that recipients of compensation be the ones harmed.

In an attempt to deny the violation of the first principle, it is sometimes argued that all blacks are the equivalent of members of a single family. While that notion may have some appeal as a symbol of solidarity, it is a pernicious notion if used here. It equates, legally and morally, individual black men and women with their racial identity. It says that race is more important than anything else in determining worth and responsibility—indeed, in determining basic identity. It is, in a word, racist.

So is its obverse, that the current generation of whites should pay for the sins of earlier generations of whites—a notion it would be necessary to enshrine in order not to violate the second principle. The current generation of whites cannot be said to be responsible for the harm inflicted by earlier generations of whites unless one elevates the principle of racial heritage to moral and legal primacy. And thus compensatory justice defenses of affirmative action fail the second principle in the same ways that they fail the first.

Socioeconomic class also becomes a factor in determining whether those injured are the ones compensated and whether those guilty are the ones who pay, for many if not most affirmative action remedies are class-bound. As to those compensated, Kent Greenawalt has written: "Even supposing wide compensation to be appropriate, admissions, job, and set-aside preferences are peculiar compensatory devices. They reach only a portion of those who are probably least harmed by earlier discrimination, that is, those who have done well enough to be applicants for admission to educational institutions or for relevant jobs or who have built up business enterprises."[26] And if the benefits of affirmative action programs are typically class- (or situation-) based, then it stands to reason that those who will pay the benefits are also class- or situation-based individuals who, presumably, are no more (and perhaps less) guilty of inflicting racial harm than other whites of their generation.

As to those who are asked to pay, John Kaplan noted over twenty years ago that the compensatory justice argument

> conceals a built-in assumption that a preference for Negroes will secure employment for them at the expense of the middle-class whites. The fact is, however, that preference for the Negro is, in today's world, discrimination against the members of those groups which are most similar to the Negro. It is the Puerto Rican, the Mexican, the Appalachian white and the American Indian who would feel the brunt of preferential treatment for the Negro.[27]

Kaplan observed that these latter groups "are least able to bear the burdens of preference for others,"[28] which is true, but the more important point is that they may be the least deserving of bearing the burdens.

The deleterious effect of employing compensatory justice arguments to defend affirmative action programs should not be minimized. Because the enforced compensation would not compensate deserving individuals—or at least not the most deserving individuals, those whom compensatory justice has identified as having been harmed in the first place—it discredits the essential justification for affirmative action. And because it would take the compensation from innocent individuals—innocent, that is, by the calculus of compensatory justice itself: those who did not cause the original harm now to be compensated—it provokes a strong sense of injustice which supports the already substantial resentment of affirmative action.

This resentment is hardly limited to uninformed or unintelligent individuals. Even critics sympathetic to affirmative action have noted its basis. As Fallon and Weiler have observed, "Preferential employment remedies typically result in the exclusion from employment opportunities of a class of persons, most often white males, who themselves may be innocent of any race-based wrongdoing. Moreover, this excluded class may comprise the relatively least advantaged whites, who may have enjoyed no personal advantages traceable to past racial injustices."[29] And it is worth quoting at some length a recently appointed member of the Supreme Court, who in a 1979 law review article forcefully articulated the objections to—and the resentment of—the compensatory justification of affirmative action.

> My father came to this country when he was a teenager. Not only had he never profited from the sweat of any black man's brow, I don't think he had ever seen a black man. There are, of course, many white ethnic groups that came to this country in great numbers relatively late in its history—Italians, Jews, Poles—who not only took no part in, and derived no profit from, the major historic suppression of the currently acknowledged minority groups, but were, in fact, themselves the object of discrimination by the dominant Anglo-Saxon majority. To be sure, in relatively recent years some or all of these groups have been the beneficiaries of discrimination against blacks, or have themselves practiced discrimination, but to compare their racial debt . . . with that of those who plied the slave trade, and who maintained a formal caste system for many years thereafter, is to confuse a mountain with a molehill. Yet curiously enough, we find that in the system of restorative justice established by the Wisdoms and the Powells and the Whites, it is precisely *these* groups that do most of the restoring. It is they who, to a disproportionate degree, are the competitors with the urban blacks and Hispanics for jobs, housing, education.[30]

Clearly, what Professor (now Justice) Scalia was referring to as "restorative justice" is what we have been calling compensatory justice. And clearly, this is a powerful rebuttal of it. The terms of the compensatory justice argument are all wrong in the affirmative action context. By those terms, Justice Scalia's father surely *was* innocent, at least relatively if not completely. Judging from his 1987 opinion in *Santa Clara County*,[31] Justice Scalia's views on this matter have not changed since he was nominated to the Supreme Court.

Indeed, Richard Posner, another widely respected intellect who was supposedly considered for the Supreme Court prior to the selection of Anthony Kennedy, made essentially the same argument as Justice Scalia. Less passionate than Scalia but no less logical, Posner wrote that "the members of the minority group who receive preferential treatment will often be those who have not been the victims of discrimination while the nonminority people excluded because of preferences are unlikely to have perpetrated, or to have in any demonstrable sense benefited from, the discrimination."[32] Had Judge Posner been elevated to the Supreme Court, he would more than likely have joined Justice Scalia in being unreceptive to defenses of affirmative action based on compensatory justice.

In sharp contrast to the arguments of compensatory justice, the central argument of this book is that proportional quotas, at least in the case of race, are justifiable in terms of distributive justice. To repeat: distributive justice as a matter of equal protection requires that individuals be awarded the positions, advantages, or benefits they would have been awarded under fair conditions. The argument I will develop is that only racism, if not of a direct and tangible sort then of an indirect and subtle sort, can explain the failure of racial minorities to attain their deserved proportion of the society's important benefits that they would have on the basis of their numbers in the society. From that, and from the assumption that racism is indisputably unfair, it follows that minorities have the right to claim proportional benefits for themselves. Later I will explain why this sort of argument is less offensive to notions of individual responsibility and entitlement.

The argument of distributive justice has a converse side, which may be the most interesting and important feature of this volume. Distributive justice also holds that individuals or groups may not claim positions, advantages, or benefits that they would not have been awarded under fair conditions. This corollary principle follows obviously from the first, if it is not a tautology: If individuals are entitled to what they would get in a fair world, then what they would not get they are not entitled to. And if an individual is solely entitled to a given benefit, then by definition another individual who also claims it is not.

This means that white individuals who would not have won for themselves a given benefit in a racially fair world, and males who would not have won a given benefit in a nonsexist world, are not entitled to claim those benefits by using putatively more objective measures of merit. If, in a fair world, white males would have achieved N percent of a given set of benefits, then white males who claim benefits beyond that percentage are claiming benefits they are not entitled to, whether or not they appear to have "earned" the benefit according to accepted criteria. The criteria are likely to be right for measuring immediate merit; they are wrong for measuring merit viewed from a larger perspective. They are wrong for measuring distributive justice. The merit claimed by these individuals is in fact a false merit because it is based on unfair competition, although the unfairness will often be undetectable—and is not their fault. And this means that white males who are disadvantaged by affirmative action programs, and who are ostensibly being discriminated against because of their race and/or gender, are in most cases not being treated unfairly at all—not, that is, being discriminated against at all. It is by this reasoning that I attempt to rebut the innocent persons argument that has so frequently, and wrongly, discredited affirmative action programs. If my analysis is correct, most of these "innocent" persons are not, although some are. This analysis provides a calculus by which we may distinguish the one from the other.

chapter I
The Central Argument

The Meaning of Racial Correlations Given
Nonracist Assumptions and Original Positions

Our central argument combines a claim of distributive justice
with a stipulated assumption about equality at birth and with deductive reasoning about subsequent departures from that equality.
The argument, in bare form, is strikingly simple, and the stipulated
assumption appears to be uncontroversial.

Let us imagine a group of newborn infants—in demographic
terms, a cohort. For purposes of simplification, let us suppose
that this cohort is roughly representative of the population of the
United States, but not precisely so. Let us say that 50 percent of the
infants in the cohort are male and 50 percent are female, and that 80
percent of the infants are white and 20 percent are black.

Now let us ask ourselves, "At the moment of birth, are there any
significant differences, aside from the obvious ones, between the
male and the female infants, or between the white and the black
infants?" To be more specific, if we could measure it accurately,
would we find statistically significant differences in the intelligence
or in the potential, as-yet-undeveloped intelligence of these subgroups? Would either the average or the range of their potential IQ's
be different—that is, would the bell-shaped curve indicating the
spread of IQ's within each group be narrower or broader for one
group, or would it center on a different point? And, let us further
ask, at this point would there be differences in their character or in
their potential character—in their ability to develop motivation,

commitment, self-discipline, desire to "get ahead," *etc.*, *etc.*? Would there, in short, be differences in their inchoate and undeveloped desires to share in all of life's promise or in their potential abilities to attain that promise?

Probably without exception, everyone asked these questions would emphatically agree that only a hard-core racist posits racial differences at birth. Most, but not all, would agree that there would be no differences between the male and the female infants at least in terms of their potential intelligence or character, but some might insist that biological differences would in and of themselves later lead to slightly different desires and motivations; and, of course, physical differences would produce different physical abilities between males and females as groups.

One has to admit that the case for absolute equality at birth is stronger with regard to race than with gender. Despite the revival several years ago by Shockley *et al.* of genetic theories of racial inferiority, not a single reputable study exists that would support a claim of general racial inferiority/superiority—in either intelligence or potential character—at birth.[1] With gender, things are somewhat more complicated. No one has seriously suggested—or rather, no one worth taking seriously has suggested—that intellectual ability *generally* or character traits *generally* differ between men and women as groups as a result of heredity. But interestingly, with the progress of feminism has come a renewed interest in, and acceptance of, biologically based differences.

This should not be surprising. When assertions of general superiority/inferiority still had a degree of respectability, and when gross "anatomy-is-destiny" generalizations still lingered, any recognition of biological differences as a source of behavioral or mental differences was both suspect and dangerous. If there is now a greater acceptance of studies attempting to link biology to gender-correlated differences in behavior and attitudes, it is doubtless because the studies have been more careful to limit their claims in terms of explanatory power and implications, and (perhaps) because it is now more possible to appreciate differences without assigning judgments of superiority or inferiority to them. To be perfectly fair, then, let us assume that reputable studies have suggested plausible biological explanations for *some* of the behavioral differences between men and women that show up at various stages of life.

While not conceding that a reputable study has ever furnished support (or likely would ever furnish support) for affirmative answers to any of the questions asked at the beginning of the chapter, let us illustrate our point using race and leave for another time the question of gender. Considering then, the two groups of infants, 80 percent white and 20 percent black, let us add a hypothetical condition. Let us imagine our cohort living in a perfectly nonracist society for, say, twenty-one years. Neither overt nor subtle discrimination has existed in this society. If there ever had been racism in the past, its effects had been completely eradicated by the time of the cohort's birth. Individuals harbor neither conscious nor unconscious racism; the color of one's skin is universally considered to be of no greater significance than, say, the color of one's hair or eyes. Role models exist for all of society's roles with equal frequencies, and in general white and black individuals are equally encouraged and discouraged by the society in whatever they undertake.

Before continuing, we should take note that a number of studies have strongly suggested that most of us treat people differently according to their physical attractiveness, even when we are not aware of it. Most of us at least initially impute greater intelligence and authority to individuals who are moderately attractive, and less to individuals who are either unattractive or conspicuously attractive. Perhaps the most disturbing studies are those that suggest that physically attractive defendants receive greater leniency than less attractive defendants. Other studies have suggested that a person's height affects how others respond to him or her. If the studies are correct, these initial judgments are usually not so strong that they withstand subsequent exposure to the individuals in question, but apparently the initial presumptions, when multiplied by the countless interactions in an individual life, have measurable cumulative effects. In the case of both attractiveness and height the studies show statistically significant correlations between these traits and success in the society.

Some would argue that such behavior is an ineradicable facet of human nature and is easily forgivable, but I would argue that it is essentially a matter of sensitivity, which can and should be taught. The important point is that such behavior does systematically reward and penalize individuals on a basis other than merit—usually on an irrelevant and immutable basis. We would therefore be justified in giving it a label corresponding to racism and sexism. Although "attractivism" and "heightism" are ungainly and off-putting neologisms unlikely to gain acceptance into our vocabulary, they would be legitimate parallel terminology. As with racism and sexism, they would identify a habit or pattern of judging people on the basis of an irrelevant accident of birth rather than on the basis of their actual individual merit. As with racism and sexism, they would be pejorative because they identify practices that violate the principle that individuals are entitled to be judged on their merit and not on the basis of irrelevant characteristics beyond their control. Thus, in all cases, the use of the terms would implicate judgments about fairness.

The point of this discursion is that even if the color of one's skin in our hypothetical society has no more significance than the color of one's hair or eyes, our society might not be perfectly nonracist, as our stipulation requires it to be. If all of us unconsciously prejudge each other, at least to some extent, on the basis of physical traits, then clearly differences in skin color present multiple opportunities for a kind of low-level racism even in a society that is not consciously racist. The discursion suggests that it will take some work to eradicate the last vestiges of racism; until a society becomes, in effect, color-blind, it cannot be sure that it is not judging people unfairly. The validity of our argument does not depend on the actual likelihood of achieving such a perfectly nonracist society, but simply on the truth of the claim that distributive justice requires thinking in terms of complete nonracism. For that reason alone, we must stipulate that in our hypothetical society the color of one's skin has absolutely no effect on people whatsoever, as if they were in fact color-blind.

The society described above is the sort of society that one would think everyone has a right to grow up in. In terms of the spirit of equal protection it is the ideal society, one where race truly is irrelevant in all aspects of life. Our claim of distributive justice is simply that one has a right to live in this sort of society or, if that is impossible, to be treated as one would have been treated in that sort of society. Distributive justice, as it relates to race, can only be determined by conceiving of the complete eradication of racism, even if that should prove to be a distant or even idle hope in practice. What is fair and what is to be realistically expected are frequently two different things, and if the one is to have any chance of influencing the other, the calculation of each must be kept separate. There is no extraordinary irony in the claim that justice in real societies is to be determined by first thinking about ideal societies.

My argument is that properly viewed, most affirmative action programs, even those which rely on so-called "hard quotas," advance this race-related claim of distributive justice; that in many situations such programs are the only way to advance the claim; and that, far from being unfair to nonminority individuals, such programs advance the claim for both disadvantaged minorities and advantaged nonminorities, both as groups and as individuals. The fact that our central reasoning could be used to indict a host of social practices and to support innumerable kinds of quotas throughout the society—that, in short, the reasoning could be pushed to the point of practical absurdity—is by itself no argument against employing it to remedy societal racism in at least those situations which seem amenable to quotas, that is, where racial disparities are stark and lack even apparent explanation.

To pursue the argument, then, let us imagine that after twenty-one years it is time for our cohort to apply to postgraduate schools. There is one medical school in this society, and it has one hundred openings for first-year students. Our twenty-one-year-olds make their decisions about what they wish to do, and then submit their applications. Central to their applications, of course, are their high school grades and, for those choosing to apply to medical school, their Medical College Admission Test (MCAT) scores.

What, we now ask, is the applicant pool at the medical school going to look like? Given our initial assumptions and our hypothetical condition of a completely nonracist society, strict logic tells us that it must look like this: The applicant pool will be 80 percent white and 20 percent black, and the hundred best qualified, as measured by high school grades and MCAT scores, will also be 80 percent white and 20 percent black.

Logic compels these answers because of what is implied by the initial assumption and by the stipulated condition. If there are no race-correlated differences in intellectual ability at birth, and no differences in character—in the inborn desire to achieve one's potential or in the potential for self-discipline to actually achieve it—then there should be no differences twenty-one years later in the racial distribution of the cohort across all of society's occupations unless they were caused by race-based societal factors, an impossibility given our stipulated condition.

That is, the racial pattern from one occupation to another should perfectly match the overall racial pattern of the cohort if the society has not favored one group and disfavored the other in the intervening twenty-one years. If the society has not in any way encouraged some and discouraged others because of their race, then there can be no other outcome than a statistically perfect match between all levels of achievement, on the one hand, and the overall racial composition of the cohort, on the other.

Indeed, there could be no statistically significant variations in any of life's activities. Suppose that it were found that the now-twenty-one-year-old blacks in the society voted at substantially lower rates than the whites. According to our logic, one would have to attribute the differential voting rates to some sort of racism. If there were no legal impediments to black voting, then one would have to conclude that the lower voting rate was a secondary or tertiary effect of racism—or, more likely, of various kinds of racism. What else, we would have to ask, could explain the differences? Why should the blacks in the cohort be less interested in politics than the whites? Or, why should they find it more inconvenient or more difficult or less rewarding to vote? The answer is that if the society were truly and thoroughly nonracist, they shouldn't, and they wouldn't.

Of Molecules and Mobility

There could also be no statistically significant variations in residence—that is, no racial patterns in housing—either from neighborhood to neighborhood or from one part of the country to another. What if a society exhibited racially distinctive residential patterns but denied the charge of continuing racism by attributing them to the lingering effects of an earlier, racist era? Suppose, to make our hypothetical society both more problematical and more like the United States—the ultimate focus of the discussion, after all—the society had once been racist, with both widespread de jure and de facto segregation, but that more than a century ago the society had promised that henceforth things would be different, had even amended its constitution to abolish at least legal racism. Now, over a hundred years later, there are widespread race-based residential differences in the society. Is it reasonable to conclude that racism continues to infect the society, or might the residential disparities be explained as "naturally continuing" without current or recent encouragement?

The answer is that after a century of putative freedom to move in pursuit of equal opportunities, racial patterns in residence can be explained only by continuing racism. Without racism blacks and whites would, over a few generations, become equal in accomplishments and motivation; in equal proportions the two groups would seek new opportunities in the cities and the suburbs, the North, the West, and the South. And without racism they would be equally welcomed and equally successful, thus encouraging, in equal measure, subsequent migrations. After several generations the only disparities would be due to the fact that a certain proportion of the population naturally stays put for many generations.

While one might think that number is substantial and would account for many disparities even after more than a century, the truth is that the American population—both white and black—has been highly mobile since the Civil War; whites have been highly mobile in almost all times and places during that period. In a recent five-year period, for instance, more than two out of every five Americans under the age of thirty-five moved. Although some moves were local—from one residence to another within the same city or town—nearly 50 percent were not: fully 10 percent of all persons in the United States moved from one state to another; 20 percent moved from one county to another. The figures for young adults are even more startling: in the same five-year period, more than two-thirds of all persons between the ages of twenty-five and thirty-four moved. And in both of the last five-year periods, more than 50 percent of the large and important segment of the population between ages twenty-five and forty-four moved.[2]

Although the figures for "repeat movers" are not available, it takes no great leap of faith to conclude that these extraordinarily high figures, repeated over several five-year periods, add up to an overwhelming population movement *even within one generation*. When multiplied by the more than five generations since the ratification of the Fourteenth Amendment, the figures strongly suggest an interesting analogy.

The American population in an ideal state—indeed, any free and relatively mobile population—can fairly be compared to a volume of gaseous molecules, in which the constant movements of the molecules result, over time, in their random redistribution. Assuming that all the molecules are equal and equally unrestricted, then no matter how they were labeled or positioned initially, there will be no pattern discernible after a certain amount of time. Assuming that black and white Americans are equal and equally influenced in their movements, then no matter what their initial status, there will be no racial patterns discernible after a certain amount of time. The implication is unavoidable: if it were not for racism, with its channeling and inhibitory effects on migration, we would not only not have ghettos and nearly white suburbs, we would also not have significant state-to-state variations, or urban-small town or north-south or east-west variations anything like the extent to which we have them now.

To be precise in our analogy we must acknowledge that not all "molecules" are equal. The patterns of mobility in the United States are nonrandom not only for race but for age, sex, and ethnicity as well as various characteristics such as educational attainment. Relatively few young people move to small midwestern towns, especially those with advanced degrees. Ditto recent immigrants from Laos. Washington, D.C., has relatively more women than men, and the reverse is true of San Diego and San Francisco.[3] But all these examples can be used to bolster our point that without racism there would be no *racial* patterns in migration.

Migration according to age and educational attainment is dependent on employment and educational opportunities, and those are determined by a number of factors which might well exist even in an ideal world: some jobs need to be near water or forests; others need to be near universities or cultural institutions, which in turn tend to be near large concentrations of people, *etc.*, *etc.* But migration according to gender is related to underlying discrimination in the society, although the precise forms may be arguable. In a society with relatively fewer professional opportunities for them, women will be attracted to cities with a large number of guaranteed equal-employment-opportunity jobs. With more than a million middle- and lower-level bureaucrats, including hundreds of thousands of traditionally female secretarial jobs as fallback opportunities, the nation's capital is a natural place for ambitious women, even as it prevents most of them from joining their brothers in the very highest ranks.

San Diego is disproportionately male because of its large military installations—which is to say, ultimately, because of Congress's (and the society's) discouragement of women in the military. San Francisco is disproportionately male because of society's widespread hostility toward homosexuals; gay men have historically sought out the anonymity of cities and the solidarity of gay subculture. As San Francisco became known as a hospitable place to live, it attracted more and more gay men, which furthered its reputation and its distinctive demographics. In an ideal world women would have no reason to prefer one city over another for professional (or personal) reasons—or rather, no reasons distinct to them as women— so whatever migration patterns existed would exist for men and women equally. Similarly, in an ideal world gay people would have no reason to resort to a subculture to feel at ease and worthy. (They might still have some reason to seek out gay neighborhoods simply because their need to meet and form special bonds with other gay individuals may be best served by a certain concentration. No rational person fishes in unpromising waters.)

Migration according to ethnicity is related to the need for continued contact with reference groups, which is in turn based at least in part on incomplete assimilation, on the larger society's failure to welcome completely the members of the ethnic group. This is doubtless understandable and forgivable in the case of very recent immigrants, especially non-Western immigrants whose language and culture are very different from the dominant American culture. But to the degree that it is not forgivable (see below), it would be removed as a determinant of migration in an ideal world, along with outright racism. Thus, in the perfectly fair society, there would still be migration disparities according to age and educational attainment, but there would be none according to gender, and few or none for ethnicity or sexual orientation.

And above all, there would be no reason for disparities based on race. Why would blacks wish to move to small-town America proportionately less frequently than whites if small-town residents welcomed blacks as warmly as they welcomed new white residents, if blacks shared the same educational and occupational characteristics, and if all of the small town's educational and occupational opportunities were available without regard to race? Whatever *other* patterns of migration would occur in an ideal world, the races would be equally distributed within them.

What, then, if there *are* race-correlated differences in any of the society's characteristics? What if we find that the applicant pool in our hypothetical medical school contains more than 80 percent whites, or that more than 80 percent of the highest-scoring applicants are white? In such a case we could only conclude that *racism had, in fact, been at work in the society* in the intervening years.

Most people would grant that such a result very strongly suggests the presence of racism but would wonder whether it is really *proof* of it. The answer must be insisted upon: if the stipulated assumption of absolute racial equality at birth is accepted, along with the stipulation of a completely nonracist society, then it is proof by the rules of deductive logic. Together, the stipulated assumptions preclude any other conclusion. If there are no relevant differences between a given group of whites and a given group of blacks at birth, then any differences manifested at a later point in their development must be the result of societal factors—i.e., racism. If not nature, then nurture.

And conversely, if there are race-correlated differences in a given population of adults and the processes of acculturation have not produced them, then the process of deduction tells us there must have been race-correlated differences at birth. If not nurture, then nature. When one finds race-based differences within a society there are but two possible explanations: racial superiority/inferiority at birth, or racism in the society. Quite simply, no other explanations are available through reason, none that conform to the laws of nature as we understand them. Divine Providence might explain why one race succeeds and another fails when both are born equal and are equally nurtured, but nothing else will.

Required Assumptions and the Court

An important broad point of constitutional interest, one having to do with modes of constitutional interpretation, should be considered here. By what right, one might ask, may the Court adopt the initial assumption of inborn racial equality employed here, and by what right may the Court read into the Equal Protection Clause its accompanying assertion that subsequent racial disparities in society must be attributed to racially disparate treatment—i.e., to racism? It is not hard to imagine critics charging the justices with extreme noninterpretivism here[4]—forsaking what can reasonably be extracted from the text and its historical documents to read into the Constitution the individual belief systems of the justices. Surely the initial assumption is merely an act of faith, however noble. And the subsequent assertion is just that: an assertion, unproven and unprovable, of either/or causality—either genetic or social determinism, or both. Even granting, *arguendo*, that the case for both may be persuasive, by what right may the Court read them into the Constitution, for surely they are but two of many plausible assumptions about racial disparities in America, none of which have any special claim to constitutional blessing.

The answer here must be in two parts. The justification for the assumption of *inborn racial equality*—or rather for its adoption by the Court—naturally begins with the essential meaning of the Equal Protection Clause. By universal agreement one of the Constitution's broader clauses, its meaning is far from self-evident. Since it doesn't actually mention race, a strictly literalist interpretation, that is, one that ignored the historical events leading up to the Fourteenth Amendment, would have trouble even showing that it forbids racial discrimination. Obviously, in interpreting this clause the Court must find its intent, its true meaning, in its historical roots and in its unstated assumptions. Any coherent interpretation—broad or narrow—of the Equal Protection Clause requires some assumption about innate racial equality or inequality.

There are only two assumptions possible here: that the races are equal at birth, or the contrary, that the races are unequal at birth. It is, in fact, easier for a Supreme Court justice to justify the assumption of inborn equality than for an average citizen because that assumption is thoroughly consistent with the spirit of the Fourteenth Amendment, especially as interpreted in the last forty years, while its opposite is thoroughly inconsistent with the amendment and would render it incoherent. Whatever the actual beliefs on the question of innate equality among the amendment's original supporters,[5] the amendment they passed, and particularly its Equal

Protection Clause, makes no sense unless it is understood as embodying an unspoken command to interpreters of it *to act as if the assumption of innate equality were true*. It is that assumption which makes discrimination fundamentally irrational and irrelevant to anything except the prejudice it was the amendment's purpose to counteract.

That is, if the races were, even in some things, inherently unequal, then discrimination according to race would sometimes be rational; as the classic formulation has it, equal protection means treating those equally situated equally and those unequally situated unequally. If race *per se* were the source of the undeniable differences that show up in society, rather than the proxy for some other causal factor like unequal education or income, then it would sometimes make a great deal of sense to treat blacks and whites differently. Because the Fourteenth Amendment is universally, and rightly, understood to be categorical in its prohibition of the use of race as a basis for *discrimination*, one can only conclude that it has declared race wholly irrelevant as a legal classification. But race is categorically irrelevant only if its only significance is skin color—that is, if the races are assumed to be inherently equal.

Either tacitly or explicitly, the Court has always reflected that assumption. It has always spoken, if not acted, as if the races are inherently equal. There has not been a single Supreme Court decision interpreting the Equal Protection Clause that can fairly be read as being based on the contrary assumption—not even the heinous *Plessy*,[6] which at least paid lip service to innate equality.

So it is not the assumption of innate equality *per se* that is difficult to justify. It is the uses to which it has been put. What may be really troublesome is the assertion that given the assumption of equality, all racial disparities in society must be attributable to racism. By what justification could the Court adopt that assertion as its own? As Richard Posner argued in the context of the *DeFunis* case[7]: "Many groups are underrepresented in various occupations for reasons of taste, opportunity, or aptitude unrelated to discrimination. There is no basis for a presumption that but for past discrimination . . . minorities . . . would supply [a proportional] percent of the nation's lawyers."[8] But Posner's own assertion, which may be taken as representative of an entire school of thought—indeed, of the conventional wisdom here—makes the same mistake of equating racial disparity with ethnically based cultural disparity that I criticized above. Such arguments can actually be used to prove the existence of racism as a not-really-similar counterpart to ethnicity. Once it is understood that there is no such thing as "racial ethnicity" without racism, Posner's assertion becomes incomprehensible without an unspoken assumption of innate black inferiority. Without that assumption there can be no *racial* underrepresentation "in various occupations for reasons of taste, opportunity, or aptitude unrelated to discrimination" because any racially correlated variation in taste, opportunity, or aptitude can *only* be explained by either innate racial differences or pervasive societal recognition of race and differential behavior based on it—i.e., *de facto* discrimination.

Contrary to what Posner and many others believe, the "basis" for the "presumption" that minorities would be proportionally represented in all occupations but for discrimination is simple: except for innate racial inferiority, there is no imaginable explanation for the contrary presumption. If all genetic and environmental explanations that take cognizance of race are ruled out—as they must be to avoid the respective charges of racism or discrimination, broadly defined—then it is hard to imagine what explanations these people have in mind.

Indeed, it is frankly impossible to conceive how anyone could make Posner's assertion and also disavow the explanation of innate racial inequality without thereby making an assertion that flies in the face of all of social science, which is predicated on the belief that behavioral differences have causes that are, broadly speaking, either genetic or environmental—and that when the former are controlled, the cause must be found among the latter. Like the so-called hard sciences, social science is deterministic in the sense that it searches for cause-and-effect relationships and doesn't accept *mystical explanations*. At least since the introduction of the Brandeis brief, the use of social science by courts has not been controversial *per se*. Judges of all kinds, interpreting laws of all kinds, routinely rely on its assumptions and methodology to establish responsibility through causality. When, as here, essentially two contrary assertions of causality are being made—the cause of racial disparity is racism; the cause is "something else"—the essential assumptions and methodologies of social science emphatically argue for the conditional acceptance of the former. A plausible, logically compelling answer is better than no answer at all, even if, like most scientific theories and all inductively reasoned conclusions, it cannot be proven in a technical sense.

Thus, while the burden of proof has universally been put on those who make the argument that racism is at the root of racial disparities in society, that burden more appropriately falls to those who assert that those disparities are somehow caused by something else. When it is claimed that neither racial inferiority nor societal factors cause racial disparities, the courts have the right, and the responsibility, to ask just what does. The burden should be on those who are currently supplying a nonanswer.

It seems that in both the assumption and the "presumption" or "assertion," there is no neutral ground for the Court. Just as the Court's interpretation of the Equal Protection Clause necessarily reflects one of two possible assumptions about inherent racial differences, so its conclusions about what right individual whites and blacks have to be treated on a racially fair basis necessarily reflect some assumption about what causes blacks as a group to behave differently from whites as a group. And as long as the Court continues to assume innate racial equality, the possible assumptions here are again essentially dual and opposite: racism is either the cause of behavioral differences or it is not; either racism or "something else."

The Court has steadfastly adopted the right assumption about inherent racial equality, the only assumption that makes sense of the overall equal protection project. But it has accepted the wrong assumption about the causes of subsequent racial disparities in society. That assumption—that there are reasons for black underachievement in society that are essentially natural and noninvidious—effectively negates the proportionality argument, that is, that blacks would attain proportional success in all of society's endeavors if they were not disproportionally hindered. The assumption, while comforting and widely shared, is not backed by reason or plausible evidence, and is ultimately wrong and invidious. The assumption most likely depends on likening race to ethnically based cultural differences, but that analogy, when analyzed, is both telling and radically inappropriate; it actually proves the case that race—pure race—is at work. Without that false equation there are no imaginable explanations for racial disparity that do not partake of race *per se*. The Court should no longer accept an unexplained assertion that the causes are "something—but nothing having to do with race." It should assume, until contrary explanations are provided, what simple reason compels: that the causes *do* have something to do with race.

Race and Cultural Ethnicity Distinguished

At this point one might object that while nature and nurture together must indeed account for all human behavior, to equate all manifestations of environmental determinism with racism goes too far; in our highly heterogeneous society, cultural variations might occur for a variety of reasons that have nothing to do with racism. In some subcultures, for instance, education is more highly valued than it is in some others, and it would be difficult to prove that racism is the only, or even a significant underlying, cause of that difference.

But the truth is that all racially correlated differences in a society can be attributed to a kind of racism—if not of a virulent and abhorrent sort, then of a subtle and only seemingly less invidious sort, a racism that might be difficult or even impossible to completely eradicate in practice but whose eradication must still be the yardstick by which racial fairness is calculated. The example of subcultures valuing education differently can, in fact, be used to illustrate the point.

Before an ethnic group can exhibit any variations with regard to the main culture, it must be an ethnic group. It must, to some degree or another, be distinguishable from the main culture. Its members must, at some level, identify each other as members, and at least some segments of the larger society must perceive them as related to each other in some way that they are not related to the larger society. Stated even more minimally, to the point of tautology, there must be something genuinely different about the group as a group. Otherwise there would be no causal explanation for the behavior difference of the group, and the correlation would be spurious and coincidental. (If there were truly no basis for identification, then, of course, there could be no "observed correlation" in the first place.)

To say, for instance, that Jewish or Asian Americans place greater value on education than does the larger society is to say that those groups of people interact in some way *as a people*. On the whole, and as a group, they influence each other on the matter of education more than others are influenced by them, and more than they are influenced by others. That is what sociologists mean when they refer to reference groups.

We are, most of us, reconciled to the existence of ethnic groups in America, and to subcultures of many sorts. Indeed, there is much to be said for them in a large, complex, and individualistic society where anomie threatens constantly. The point, however, is simply that ethnicity *does exist*. And if it didn't, then neither would ethnic differences and ethnically based correlations. If blacks were merely an ethnic rather than a racial group, and if there were differences between them as a group and the larger society, then we would have to conclude that their "ethnicity" meant something, that it had its effects, that it explained those differences. Race, here, is nothing more than ethnicity with color. Racial self-identification and social identification of racial groups exist just as ethnic self-identification and social identification of ethnic groups exist. And just as those identifications are the source and explanation of ethnically based differences, so are the racial identifications the source and explanation of all race-based differences.

As with ethnicity, a certain degree of racial self-identification might appear to be a good thing. It provides special support and validation in an intimidating and impersonal universe. But also as with ethnicity, racial self-identification means incomplete assimilation. Ethnicity is intrinsically good, if it is good at all, for one reason only. Because there is no single, or obvious, best way of doing most of the thousands of things that a culture does, the general culture profits from the ferment, from the choices provided by ethnic richness and variety. Cultural variation is thus natural, inevitable, evolutionarily useful, and often free of moral significance.

But ethnicity also has a bad side. Too often it is a manifestation of the group's exclusion and defensiveness. To a too-great extent it is but a compensating good for the group; it provides a fallback reference when the society fails to completely welcome the members of the group into the larger society. It provides the individual and group with a validation that the larger society withholds.

It is possible, but just barely, to conceive of an ideal society with ethnic differences (and hence ethnicity, the recognition of ethnic reference groups by the groups and by those outside the groups). In a truly ideal world reference groups would probably not even be necessary, since the larger society, if it were in fact perfect, would provide a sufficient basis for individual-group identification; it would prevent individuals from becoming isolated and alienated. But if reference groups did exist, they would be voluntary, affirmative rather than defensive, and fluid. They would be chosen on an *ad hoc* basis and discarded when they no longer served the interests of the individuals who chose them.

In an ideal world ethnicity would reflect only the appeal of tradition—not "one's tradition" but tradition *per se*—and the respect for history—again, not one's own history so much as the richness and inherent importance of history itself. Ethnicity would be an affirmation of different heritages, all equally valid and valuable, all welcomed into and subsumed under a larger heritage. It would have roughly as much utility and strength as neighborhood or professional associations, and the degree to which an individual participated in ethnic self-identification and association would be at least as voluntary and fluctuating as it is in those and other voluntary associations.

Whatever positive value ethnic self-awareness might have, the critical point here is this: unlike ethnicity, *the race-based counterpart of ethnicity can have no inherently positive aspects*. It can have only the negative, defensive, and compensatory characteristics of reference groups. Racial self-identification and social recognition of racial groups cannot have inherent value unless race *per se* has social value in the same way that ethnic cultural variation does. If no significance attaches to race *per se*, then racial self-identification can only be that fallback reference made necessary by the society's failure to accept the members of the group on a race-blind basis. It can only signify the incomplete acceptance of the racial group into the society. In short, racial self-identification can only prove that racial characteristics in and of themselves still carry some significance in the society—which is to say that the society is still racist.

Contrary to what many commentators apparently think, there is no such thing as "racial ethnicity" without racism. The unexamined equation of race and ethnicity—the implicit use of the concept of "racial ethnicity"—underlies much of Thomas Sowell's influential attack on affirmative action, for instance. Sowell's writings are worth examining at some length because they are something of a "classic" in the affirmative action debate, and because they constitute as sustained a rejection of the argument presented here as it is possible to imagine.[9] Sowell's essential argument is that because most measures of success in society are dependent on age and geographical location, among other things, and because there are significant differences in the median age and geographical distribution of blacks and whites as groups, we cannot assume that black underrepresentation in a given occupation (or income group or educational level, etc., etc.) is a result of "discrimination."

Sowell has marshaled impressive evidence that blacks and whites do, indeed, differ in these matters, and it is true that an accurate portrait of *overt* discrimination would have to control for these differences. For instance, it is incorrect to assert that overt discrimination against blacks accounts for all the disparity in black family income (62 percent of the national average) when income is so dependent on age, education, and geographical location, for blacks as a group are younger, less educated, and disproportionately located in lower-income areas of the country. The implication is that blacks and whites of the same age and education and living in the same place would earn roughly the same incomes. But the question is why blacks taken as a whole should differ from whites in terms of these basic, intervening variables. Our answer is that if it weren't for the deeper, subtler, systematic racism in the society, they wouldn't.

Sowell's answer is to compare blacks with ethnic groups. His identification of blacks with ethnic groups supports his argument that what distinguishes blacks from whites in America today is essentially their cultural differences rather than their skin color. Even without discrimination, he argued, blacks would exhibit cultural variations such as "historic differences that existed before they ever set foot on American soil." As examples of such differences he cited "the overrepresentation of Jews in the clothing industry, Germans in the beer industry, or the Irish in politics and the priesthood."[10] It turns out that even after controlling for age, education, and geographical residence, blacks do not earn as much as whites. So one must also control for "reading (or nonreading) habits." Thus, "the still large racial income difference was cultural rather than racial, as such."[11]

But again, one must ask why blacks as a group have different reading habits than whites do. Why should blacks exhibit any cultural pattern different from white culture? And if Sowell's essential argument is to hold up, one condition must be met: black culture must be assumed to be naturally "inherited" and unrelated to the larger society's prejudice or discrimination. Otherwise, Sowell would have to acknowledge that racism is at least one cause of the cultural differences that in turn "explain" many of the socioeconomic differences between blacks and whites. To acknowledge that would be largely to blunt the major thrust of his attack on the "presuppositions of affirmative action" that but for racism, blacks would experience rates of success and failure in all things equal to whites.

It is telling in the extreme, then, that even two out of three of Sowell's own examples of ethnic variation implicate prejudice and hostility. If nineteenth-century Jewish immigrants were overrepresented in the clothing industry, it surely was due in part to their exclusion, in Europe and America, from many of the rest of society's occupations. And if Irish Americans took to politics with special enthusiasm it was surely due in part to their perceived need to protect themselves from the larger, Protestant society. Along with other examples used by Sowell, these two actually undermine the argument for naturally occurring diversity, that is, diversity in the absence of discrimination or prejudice. As I am about to argue, true reference groups are almost always accompanied by the sort of value judgments that underpin prejudice and discrimination.

It is undeniable that the predominant, contemporary white culture diverges in numerous and important ways from much of contemporary black culture, but it is not plausible, as Sowell would apparently have us believe, that those differences are not maintained and promoted by racial consciousness *per se*. It is not plausible that those differences would be just as pronounced if people had been literally color-blind since the first blacks arrived in America. It strains credulity to believe that blacks as a group would be so distinct from mainstream society, so unintegrated into it, if they had been able to "pass" as white throughout their long history in America. That history, after all, is substantially longer than that of any other immigrant group except the original colonists—and essentially equal to theirs. If cultural assimilation is a function of time, as history shows that it generally is, then even the most distinctive traits of African cultures would have been long since *adopted or rejected by the whole culture* if blacks had simply had Caucasian features. And all those aspects of contemporary black culture that are not rooted in the Africa of then or now—"reading (or nonreading) habits," *etc.*—could never have developed in the first place, at least not as *racial* characteristics.

In an ideal world race would truly mean nothing. It would be no basis for group identification, and hence no basis for group correlations, so that race-based correlations could not exist. Even if it is true that everyone in a society as complex as ours needs reference groups, blacks would be dispersed randomly into other reference groups. If the society were not racist, some blacks would identify themselves as midwesterners, or as good bowlers, Methodists, dentists, overweight, tall, violinists, cross-dressing Republicans, *etc.*, *etc.* But they would no more identify themselves as blacks than others would identify themselves as brown-eyed, and there would be no more race-correlated differences in the society than there are eye-color-correlated differences now.[12]

As a practical matter, it may seem both radical and naïve to insist that in an ideal world there would not be the slightest recognition of race. Many people who do not consider themselves racist would find nothing very objectionable in blacks forming reference groups at least to the same extent as, say, midwesterners or tall persons do. Assuming that the society attaches no superiority or inferiority to these characteristics, what harm can there be in recognizing a shared physical trait and in identifying to a slight extent with those who share the trait?

But in the first place, few, if any, of the common bases of reference groups are truly neutral in terms of judgments of superiority/inferiority (like the "heightism" mentioned earlier), which means that few, if any, of them are without significant social effects. To the extent that midwesterners really *identify* themselves as such—psychologically, as opposed to merely using the term descriptively—it reflects a sense of *significant*, not trivial, difference from, and often a degree of superiority to, someone else (most likely New Yorkers or Californians). Non-midwesterners who actually think of others as midwesterners—again, as opposed to merely describing them as such—are also thinking in terms of significant differences, typically in terms of cultural inferiority. The fact that there are exceptions to the generalization—that some midwesterners may feel inferior to non-midwesterners and some non-midwesterners may romantically assign to midwesterners superior virtue—only strengthens the point. True reference groups do not form until *identification* occurs, as opposed to mere description. But once identification has gone past the point of mere description it is rarely neutral. Even putatively descriptive-only identifications often carry subconscious judgments with them.

Probably we will never be able to eradicate stereotypical thinking in all its manifestations, and probably we would not want to eliminate it completely, since it can be both efficient and innocuous. The question is whether we wish to completely eradicate *racial* stereotyping. If we do, then we must be clear-headed that nothing here is truly innocuous. Racially based reference groups are a sure signal that racial stereotyping still exists. If blacks were to form genuine reference groups, it could only signify—well, *significance*: that race *means* something, that the races are significantly different, either *per se* or derivatorily because people believe they are and act as if they are. Race-based reference groups would almost surely mean that minorities still felt a degree of separateness, of difference, of exclusion, from the larger society.

Indeed, some of our reluctance to banish minority racial reference groups surely stems from our perception of them as protective and defensive. We would hesitate to abolish them even if we could because we don't really believe complete assimilation is possible. With incomplete assimilation and no reference groups, black individuals would be especially vulnerable to psychological, if not social and economic, harm. In hesitating to endorse the complete eradication of racial sensibility, we are most likely reacting to an image of minorities atomized and rendered defenseless against the racially cohesive larger society. But, of course, if our stipulations are taken seriously, the larger society would not be "racially cohesive." It would not even be aware of minorities as such, and would not—could not—victimize them in any way on the basis of their race.

In a still-racist society, however, where minorities are deprived of critical psychological and social defense mechanisms, racial minorities must have some identity to affirm their worth. For example, members of the National Association of Black Social Workers oppose adoption of black children by white parents because they "consider transracial adoption a form of cultural and racial genocide" which leads "to psychological problems in adolescence and adulthood."[13] This is precisely the sort of fear that arises when reasonable people are presented with the prospect of a society without minority reference groups. The NABSW's concern is that black children will be prevented from identifying with blacks, and that when the inevitable racism affects them, they will have no one to affirm their worth. Indeed, until racism is completely abolished, the breakdown of black solidarity, in whatever form, is quite dangerous to blacks in general. But in a hypothetical ideal society in which racism had been completely abolished, black solidarity would be neither dangerous nor necessary. It would, however, be anachronistic.

Must Black Pride be abolished, then? Should the affirmation that "black is beautiful" be discouraged? It depends. The answer is no as long as there is the slightest reason not to be as proud of being black as one would be of being white, as long as there is the slightest doubt that black is as beautiful as white is. But stated this way, the real answer is obviously yes once racism has been abolished. Why should there be pride in one's race at all if its essential worthiness is not in question? Why should one's skin color be praised if it is not maligned? Racial pride is positive—as it undeniably is for disadvantaged minorities—only in the context of racism.

chapter II
The Innocent Persons
Argument Examined

The Innocent Person Shown to Be Guilty
When Claiming Proportional Set-Aside Positions

The genuinely radical import of this exercise in logic is that accepting the nonracist premise of true equality at birth requires the conclusion that racism directly or indirectly accounts for all the behavioral and attitudinal differences between whites and blacks as groups, including all that are relevant to the attainment of the society's generally recognized goods. And the significance of that for at least some real-world affirmative action programs is apparent. The facts of our hypothetical situation were, of course, chosen because they suggest the facts of *Regents of the University of California v. Bakke*,[1] the famous first affirmative action case the Supreme Court decided. *Was* Allan Bakke, as a majority of justices held over a dozen years ago, entitled to be admitted because his high school record and MCAT scores were better than those of the minority applicants the University of California at Davis admitted? Did he have a right to have his admission decision be based on those factors to the exclusion of racial factors—that is, did he have a right to have his admission decided without regard to his race? Would he have been unfairly discriminated against if he had not been admitted? The answer to all these questions, given this broader perspective, is emphatically not.

If, as the *Bakke* briefs stipulated, California's minority population then was roughly 22 percent and yet only a few percent of Davis's top hundred applicants were minorities, then either those minorities were at birth seriously inferior in terms of innate intellect or motivation (or both), or something was dreadfully wrong with California society in the decades before the *Bakke* case. And as suggested earlier, only a hard-core racist would maintain that the former was the case rather than the latter. In a more perfect world those minority applicants would have achieved superior high school records and MCAT scores in proportion to their percentage of the general population. And in that more perfect world, *Bakke's so-called objective record would have placed him below the top one hundred candidates.* Bakke apparently would have ranked among the top hundred white applicants, but he would not have ranked among the top hundred of *all* candidates. To reward Bakke by admitting him instead of a minority candidate was to allow him to reap one of the rewards of society's racism.

In a just society the sons and daughters would not be permitted to reap the rewards of the sins of their parents. Bakke had no right to that seat in the first-year class because in the absence of racism it would have been fairly won by a minority applicant. Bakke should have been allowed to compete only for the percentage of seats that his group would have won in a nonracist society; if the briefs in the *Bakke* case were correct, that would mean that to be fairly admitted he would have had to rank among the top seventy-eight white applicants. As it turns out, the university had been generous (with someone else's rights) in allowing him to compete for eighty-four of the one hundred seats.

The argument up to this point can be generalized, if somewhat awkwardly. An affirmative action program does not violate the rights of innocent white individuals when it guarantees to minorities the portion of society's goods that minority individuals would have gained for themselves in a nonracist environment. Even a rigid quota does not violate the rights of whites when the quota does not exceed the portion of the benefit in question that would have gone to minority individuals under conditions of fair competition and given nonracist assumptions about innate equality. Individuals who have not personally harmed minorities may nevertheless be prevented from reaping the benefits of the harm inflicted by the society at large. There is no violation of equal protection when society acts to restore the equilibrium that would have naturally occurred under nonracist conditions. Indeed, to fail to maintain the equilibrium by using final-stage measures of merit is to allow the processes of racism to culminate in their inevitable inequities. In the process, white individuals would receive unearned benefits even though they had not personally caused the disequilibrium—even though, that is, they were not personally guilty of racism.

The Innocent Persons Argument and the Court

As one commentator has noted, the Supreme Court has made occasional remarks that racism has produced windfalls for whites, who, the Court has implied, had reached their present place only by preventing racial minorities from competing with them.[2] Unfortunately, the "occasional remarks" have been only that; they have never risen to the level of a sustained, or even serious, argument. Thus, for instance, even in *Bakke* four justices hinted that whites forced to apply for proportional set-aside positions would not qualify for those positions under nonracist conditions:

> If it was reasonable to conclude—as we hold that it was—that the failure of minorities to qualify for admission at Davis under regular procedures was due principally to the effects of past discrimination, then there is a reasonable likelihood that, but for pervasive racial discrimination, respondent [i.e., Bakke] would have failed to qualify for admission even in the absence of Davis's special admissions program.[3]

The clear sense of this passage is that under fair conditions minorities would have naturally infiltrated, as it were, the ranks of high-scoring candidates in numbers such that Bakke would have ranked below the cutoff line. This is as close as any members of the Court have come to adopting this book's central argument, yet it tantalizes more than it persuades. It fails to suggest a genuine, independent defense of affirmative action because of its brevity (the quoted passage is the entire argument), its tentative and qualified language, and its failure to draw the important conclusion that Bakke and all individuals situated like him thus have no moral claim to the benefits in question. Without that explicit conclusion, the passage, and the entire opinion, fail to deflect the argument that Bakke was discriminated against unfairly. Given these failings, it is perhaps not surprising that the argument—however great its potential—was never pursued in subsequent decisions.

The result of the failure to pursue the argument, however, has been that every member of the pre-Richmond Court seemed to have endorsed the innocent persons argument, if in some cases only by default. As indicated above, there are differences in the degree to which, and the purposes for which, the justices employed it, but no one seems to have found a way to rebut it. As Sullivan has noted,

> The Court has never held whites' "innocence" to be an absolute bar to affirmative action that would comparatively disadvantage them. On the contrary, even Justice Powell's opinion in *Wygant* took the Court to be in consensus that, "[a]s part of this Nation's dedication to eradicating racial discrimination, innocent persons may be called upon to bear some of the burden of the remedy."[4]

Of the pre-1989 justices, two endorsed the innocent persons argument most explicitly and enthusiastically and employed it unconditionally to attack virtually any use of affirmative action, Justice Powell's claim of consensus notwithstanding. Another three justices endorsed the argument generally but employed it only when the affirmative action program involved quotas and/or when the harm to the "innocent persons" was especially severe. Another three justices seem to have endorsed the argument tacitly and begrudgingly while denigrating its significance. A final pre-Richmond justice appears to fall in this latter category despite an unusual disclaimer.

Chief Justice Rehnquist and Justice Scalia have never upheld the use of a racial or sexual quota, in large part because of their belief that white males are always unfairly victimized by them and that such victimization is never constitutionally permissible.[5] At the other extreme are three justices who, while not denying the innocence of white males displaced by affirmative action programs, have tended to minimize the importance of their claims. In *Bakke*, Justices Brennan, Marshall, and Blackmun acknowledged "our deep belief that 'legal burdens should bear some relationship to individual responsibility or wrongdoing,'" and repeated the warning from Justice Brennan's concurrence in *United Jewish Organizations v. Carey*[6] that "the 'natural consequence of our governing processes [may well be] that the most "discrete and insular" of whites [will] be called upon to bear the immediate, direct costs of benign discrimination' "—but then simply proceeded to declare that "Davis' articulated purpose of remedying the effects of past societal discrimination is, under our cases, sufficiently important to justify the use of race-conscious admissions programs where there is a sound basis for concluding that minority underrepresentation is substantial and chronic, and that the handicap of past discrimination is impeding access of minorities to the medical school."[7]

In other words, the harm to innocent (and politically powerless) persons is regrettable, but the compelling end justifies the means. The only other reference to the innocent persons argument in Justice Brennan's *Bakke* opinion is an even more explicit denigration of it. Referring to *Franks v. Bowman Transportation Company*,[8] in which the Court had awarded the seniority he would have had without discrimination ("constructive seniority") to a victim of discrimination, placing him ahead of white workers who were not responsible for the discrimination, Justice Brennan wrote: "[the] claims of those burdened by the race-conscious actions of a university or employer who has never been adjudged in violation of an anti-discrimination law are not any more or less entitled to deference than the claims of the burdened nonminority workers in *Franks* . . . , for in each case the employees are innocent of past discrimination."[9] Since the Court in *Franks* had ultimately shown no "deference" to the claims of the innocent employees, the effect is to ask, Why the special concern now? In short, the opinions of these justices strongly suggest the principle that whenever the claims of innocent white males conflict with the claims of victimized minorities, the latter take precedence.

Justice White was the fourth member of the "liberal" plurality in *Bakke*, so the interpretation above can arguably be applied to his position as well. He also voted to uphold the voluntary quota in *Weber*.[10] But in *Santa Clara County*[11] he indicated that he would now vote to overrule *Weber*, at least, on the ground that it has been interpreted by the majority to permit the imposition of quotas too routinely.[12] Notwithstanding *Bakke*, White's position appears to be that preferential hiring and promotion are acceptable only when the employer has been guilty of past discrimination, and even then, the preferential treatment must not take the form of a "strict racial quota." When the employer has not been found guilty of discrimination, passing over innocent white workers for promotions or refusing to hire them in the first place—or laying them off ahead of less-senior minority workers—are "impermissible remed[ies]" because they are simply too "inequitable."[13]

There is at least a degree of illogic in Justice White's position because, as Justice Brennan's citation to *Franks* indicates, even imposing affirmative action when the employer has been guilty permits a degree of harm to white employees "innocent of past discrimination." To be even that consistent, of course, Justice White would have to repudiate the opinion he joined in *Bakke*, for it is not clear why universities innocent of past discrimination should be able to impose quotas on their entering students while innocent employers may not impose quotas on their workers. But the point here is that Justice White seems to have acknowledged the innocence in all cases; he simply elevated it to the level of inviolability in some cases and subordinated it in others.

Both Justice O'Connor and Justice Powell have upheld affirmative action programs, but their criteria are different. Justice O'Connor has been outspoken in rejecting the idea that generalized racial proportionality is a valid benchmark and justification for affirmative action quotas in particular cases. Justice O'Connor believes that it is unrealistic to think that individuals of any race would "gravitate with mathematical exactitude to each employer or union absent unlawful discrimination."[14] It is also sheer speculation, according to Justice O'Connor, to determine "how many minority students would have been admitted to the medical school at Davis absent past discrimination in educational opportunities."[15]

The two arguments—ideal-world racial proportionality and innocent persons—are logically bound together because the rights of white individuals *would* be violated if racial proportionality did not occur in the absence of discrimination. (And, conversely, if racial proportionality did naturally occur, then the displaced white individuals had no right to the benefit in question in the first place.) Not surprisingly, then, Justice O'Connor is of the belief that quotas always violate the rights of innocent individuals.[16] Like Justice White, she has emphasized the difference between "hard quotas" and "flexible goals." The programs she has approved have been characterized—at least by her[17]—as employing the latter rather than the former.

Justice Powell upheld affirmative action programs only when he was convinced that the harm to innocent persons was relatively light and diffuse.[18] He remained of the belief that quotas "almost invariably affect some innocent persons"[19] but voted to override the claims of those persons in the name of affirmative action when the harm to them was "diffused among society generally" or "over a period of time,"[20] a distinction that seems to lack foundation in a neutral principle.

Justice Stevens's position on the innocent persons argument is perhaps the most elusive. On the one hand, in a 1987 case he argued that the Civil Rights Act of 1964 should have been interpreted to prohibit all race- or gender-conscious programs. While it is possible to hold to this statutory interpretation without also accepting the innocent persons argument which surely infuses it, Justice Stevens's emphasis on the protection this interpretation would afford white males strongly suggests that he thought these people essentially innocent.[21] But noting that "the Court [has not] adhered to that construction of the Act," that cases like *Bakke* and *Weber* holding the contrary "are now an important part of the fabric of our law," and that "there is an undoubted public interest in 'stability and orderly development of the law,'" the justice proceeded to justify the contrary interpretation in language among the most sweeping the Court has seen.[22] That justification is of a piece with his opinion in *Paradise*—an Equal Protection Clause case— which to most observers is an even stronger, less conditional grant of authority to federal judges to impose quotas than is Justice Brennan's plurality opinion.

Thus, before *Richmond*, Justice Stevens seemed to be in the camp of those most supportive of quotas while saying that, at least as a matter of statutory interpretation, they are impermissible. But in *Richmond* he joined in striking down the city's quota, in large part because it benefited more than the actual victims of discrimination and harmed more than the actual perpetrators of discrimination. He also found the law "equally vulnerable" because it failed to identify the characteristics of the disadvantaged class of white contractors, a class that "unquestionably includes some white contractors who are guilty of past discrimination against blacks," but which also "presumably includes some who have never discriminated against anyone on the basis of race." For Stevens, "Imposing a common burden on such a disparate class merely because each member of the class is of the same race stems from reliance on a stereotype rather than fact or reason."[23] Thus emphasis on specific victims and perpetrators is consistent with a rejection of racial proportionality and an acceptance of the innocent persons argument, and Justice Stevens's language in Richmond leaves no doubt, finally, where he stands on that issue.

Thus, with varying degrees of enthusiasm—and drawing different conclusions—the entire pre-Richmond Court seemed to have accepted the argument that affirmative action programs punish the innocent. Given that, what is surprising is that a decision like Richmond was not handed down sooner. Justice Kennedy's brief concurrence in that case suggests his opposition to virtually all affirmative action programs involving racial goals or quotas. He indicated a preference for Justice Scalia's "rule of automatic invalidity for racial preferences in almost every case," but out of respect for precedent he accepted Justice O'Connor's rule that "any racial preference must face the most rigorous scrutiny by the courts." The latter, he thought, would suffice "because it forbids the use even of narrowly drawn racial classifications except as a last resort."[24]

However, even if Justice Powell had remained on the Court and had voted to uphold the Richmond ordinance on the grounds that the harm to innocent white contractors was sufficiently "diffuse" (a far from certain speculation), there would have been enough votes on the Court to strike it down and reject the use of generalized racial proportionality as a justification of particular quotas—which is exactly what the Richmond Court did. Given the Court's failure to rebut the innocent persons argument, it may have been only a matter of time before a majority would begin finding rigid quotas unacceptable.

The Misplaced Emphasis on Innocence and Blame

As one recent commentator has noted, the Court's approach has actually invited the argument that affirmative action programs punish innocent whites. Whether upholding or attacking affirmative action, the Court has "[cast] affirmative action as penance for particular sins of discrimination," and "because corrective justice focuses on victims, and retributive justice on wrongdoers, predicating affirmative action on past sins of discrimination invites claims that neither nonvictims should benefit, nor nonsinners pay."[25] If our central argument is correct, however, questions of innocence and blame are fundamentally irrelevant in affirmative action cases, and the controlling question is always one of equity.

The goal in these cases, as in equal protection cases involving race generally, is to prevent unfairness to minority individuals while at the same time preventing unfairness to nonminority individuals. And, as in matters of equity generally, the proper focus of injury is not on questions of guilt or innocence *per se*—they are the usual but not universal secondary questions—but on questions of right: Who is entitled to what? If the basic inquiry in affirmative action cases is what members of a racial group would receive had they not been victimized by racism, then the question is not Who is to blame for the racism? but What would the group members have naturally attained? And when the inquiry turns to fairness to white individuals, the question is not whether they have been guilty of racism in the given instance but, again, what they would be entitled to in a nonracist society.[26]

It is true that questions of right frequently hinge on questions of personal guilt and innocence. When a party is found guilty of relevant and impermissible behavior, it typically causes his or her claim of right to be *ipso facto* forfeited or negated. But almost as frequently, personal guilt or innocence is irrelevant to the claim of right, as when a party innocently comes into possession of stolen goods; the claim on those goods by the rightful owner is not forfeited because of the innocence of the current possessor. The error of certain members of the Court has been to apply one rule from the law of equity where another should have been used.

Suppose, for instance, that what was "dreadfully wrong with California society in the decades before the *Bakke* case" was somehow not the government's fault. It is probably impossible to imagine an actual scenario in which the government of California would not in some degree be guilty, especially if one considers the state to have an affirmative duty to eradicate the causes and effects of racism wherever and whenever it can, but let us assume *arguendo* that California is somehow not at fault for this disparity in achievement between two groups of its citizens where there should be no disparity. How does that affect the rights of the Davis applicants? The answer is: not at all. Once it is granted that the members of each racial group are entitled to compete for the share of a benefit that the group would have obtained through natural competition in a nonracist society, the cause of the distorted competition becomes irrelevant and does not affect the claims of either group. As a matter of both law and equity, a party's claim to what is rightfully his or hers is not affected by whether it was taken from him or her by the party who now wishes to take possession of it or by a third party. And, of course, the party who would now wrongfully possess a thing has no greater claim to it just because it was stolen by a third party, even though the former would be legally and morally innocent if there was no way of knowing that the thing was stolen.

By the same token, the duties of the Davis Medical School admissions committee would not change. If it is granted that members of a group are entitled to the share of entering places that the group would have received in the absence of racism, then it follows that the admissions committee may not be relieved of its duty to allot that share just because neither it nor its parent, the state, caused the racism. If judges do not legitimize theft because the wrongful claimant is not the thief, and if courts do not refuse to make whole a victim because the process of victimization had multiple stages, then the admissions committee may not close its eyes to the injustice that has been done merely because the committee was not itself the source of the injustice.

It follows from this that the Reagan administration and certain justices were flat wrong when they insisted that affirmative action programs are unconstitutional violations of equal protection if they operate to take away a "right" or benefit from an individual who has not personally discriminated against the victim(s). The Reagan administration's view is represented by its endorsement of Justice Stewart's argument in *Fullilove* that ordinarily "the guarantee of equal protection prohibits the government from taking detrimental action against innocent people on the basis of the sins of others of their own race."[27] The administration's argument in *Wygant* was that white workers are virtually always innocent of the sin of past discrimination practiced by their bosses or their union leadership, and hence cannot be made to bear the burden of affirmative action hiring quotas.

Was Allan Bakke personally responsible for any of the racism that held back the minority applicants? Very possibly not, but that is the wrong question. That makes him "innocent" only *up to the point at which he applies for one of the special admission seats.* But he becomes a guilty party the moment he seeks to receive a benefit he would not qualify for without the accumulated effects of racism. At that point he becomes an accomplice in, and a beneficiary of, society's racism. He becomes the recipient of stolen goods. By most accounts his moral culpability would depend on the degree to which he knew, or could have known, that the benefit in question was not his to apply for, and we may readily grant that Bakke and many others could sincerely and intelligently believe that that was not the case. But Bakke's innocent motivation is no reason to reward him. If the benefit is not rightly his, it is not rightly his, period, regardless of whether he personally caused any minority individuals to not apply or any minority applicants to score below their innate potential. To deny the benefit to him would be no more unjust than it would be to deny him the right to sift through and claim stolen goods.

By the same token, the Reagan administration and certain members of the Court were also wrong in insisting that affirmative action programs must be limited to restoring rights to individuals who can prove that they have been *personally* injured by the party implementing the program. The administration first advanced the argument that "preferential" treatment may be extended "only to the actual victims of discrimination"—by which the administration meant individuals who could, almost literally, point to specific acts of discrimination against them personally by the targeted entity—in *Firefighters v. Stotts.*[28] Claiming that *Stotts* had upheld their "proposition," the administration repeated the argument in each of the three affirmative action cases decided in 1986.[29] Finally, while those cases were pending, the administration made the argument again in seeking certiorari in *United States v. Paradise.*[30] By a 6–3 majority the Court rejected at least the extreme of this argument. It found "victim specificity" neither a constitutional nor a statutory (Title VII) requirement, at least when "an employer or labor union has engaged in persistent or egregious discrimination, or where necessary to dissipate the lingering effects of pervasive discrimination."[31] Yet because of the Court's apparent emphasis on exceptional circumstances, it remained uncertain just when non-victim-specific plans could be employed.[32]

Would a generalized underrepresentation of minorities be sufficient to justify "preferential treatment" of minority individuals who could not show specific victimization? In 1987, in *Johnson v. Santa Clara County*, the Court upheld a voluntary affirmative action program by a government agency that had "identified a conspicuous imbalance in job categories traditionally segregated by race and sex," while emphasizing that the program did not involve rigid quotas.[33] Thus the only non-victim-specific remedy that seems still prohibited is a judicially imposed "hard quota" when there has been no showing of "egregious" or "pervasive" discrimination by the target of the order. Whether or not Solicitor General Charles Fried was correct in his assessment of the earlier cases, the Court now seems to have said: "Not always, but more often than not." This time the dissenters were Justices Rehnquist, White, and Scalia.

The proper perspective again shows why the "victim-specific" argument is also wrong. Once it is granted that the set-aside seats in Davis's entering class cannot rightfully go to any nonminority candidate but instead must go to some minority applicant, the only remaining question is which minority candidates are entitled to those seats. And the question of racial fairness having been thus disposed of, it is not unreasonable to reimpose the standard measures of merit: high school records, recommendations, MCAT scores, interviews, *etc*. The objection that affirmative action quotas like this act to reward undeserving minority individuals has little force if the standard is the same for minority individuals and nonminority individuals: who among your group is the best and the brightest? If it can be reasonably shown that minority individuals would have won at least sixteen of the one hundred seats in Davis's freshman class, then those judged to be the sixteen best-qualified minority applicants are in a very real sense entitled to them. Indeed, only by using quotas in these situations can true individual merit be rewarded, for if the University of California's goal is to admit the best and brightest of all the state's people, then it can only do so by taking into account the fact that all of its racial subgroups will have the same proportion of society's best and brightest.

But even if it should sometimes prove impossible to identify the theoretically deserving individuals—that is, to know with confidence which minority individuals would have qualified for the benefit in question in a nonracist society—the rights of the white individuals will be affected only marginally, if at all. Their claim will already have been disposed of. Even if the most deserving black individual does not get the benefit, whites' claim to the benefit does not suddenly become legitimate. When the rightful owner of stolen goods cannot be found, the law—which is to say, the government—may or may not award possession to the original but wrongful claimant; but if it does not, if it awards possession to a third party whose claim is arguable, the original claimant cannot justifiably feel morally harmed. And the government's action cannot be said to be arbitrary unless it awards the goods to an individual whose claim is even less plausible than that of the original claimant. That can never be the case in affirmative action cases involving proportional quotas, because any minority individual has a better claim than any white individual has—which is no claim at all.

This is, I think, at least a partial response to the challenge from George Sher, who concluded his own defense of "reverse discrimination" this way:

> If the point of reverse discrimination is to compensate for competitive disadvantages caused by past discrimination, it will be justified in favor of only those group members whose abilities have actually been reduced; and it would be most implausible to suppose that *every* black . . . has been affected in this way. Blacks from middle-class or affluent backgrounds will surely have escaped many, if not all, of the competitive handicaps besetting those raised under less fortunate circumstances; and if they have, our account provides no reason to practice reverse discrimination in their favor. Again, whites from impoverished backgrounds may suffer many, if not all, of the competitive handicaps besetting their black counterparts; and if they do, the account provides no reason *not* to practice reverse discrimination in their favor. Generally, the proposed account allows us to view racial . . . boundaries only as roughly suggesting which individuals are likely to have been disadvantaged by past discrimination. Anyone who construes these boundaries as playing a different and more decisive role must show us that a different defense of reverse discrimination is plausible.[34]

This is a forceful statement of the conventional wisdom, but I believe it is incorrect. It confuses racial fairness with a more generalized socioeconomic fairness, and would in effect require the former to be sacrificed to the latter rather than addressing the latter as an independent wrong. If, under conditions of fairness, society exhibits racial proportionality in all things, then individual rights can be at least initially calculated by reference to racial ratios. One of the outer perimeters, if you will, of individual rights can be calculated by referring to proportionality. Reference to racial ratios can (usually) tell us when a white individual has no claim whatsoever to a benefit. That being true, it is irrelevant to the question of racial fairness whether the white individual has been disadvantaged relative to other whites; she or he still has no claim to something that in a fair world would go to some black individual.

That may sound callous; it is not intended to be. Surely, unfairness to poor whites is a serious matter in its own right—so serious that one cannot say that it is a lesser injustice than racial injustice. But the point is that it is a *different* injustice, and the net unfairness of the society is not improved by giving to poor whites what blacks would have won under racially fair conditions. The disadvantaging of whites by an unfair socioeconomic system should be independently addressed; and so should the possible benefit already advantaged blacks might gain by the imposition of racially fair quotas: If some blacks profit who shouldn't, the culprit is class inequality, not racial fairness. The only proper remedy for both kinds of class-based unfairness is one that addresses class *per se*, not its frequent proxy, race.

Sher's argument, often repeated on the Supreme Court, winds up making racial fairness and social fairness compete with each other in the context of doubly inadequate benefits; it forces them to be falsely antagonistic. They are not, and should not be, antagonistic. Rather, each claim deserves to be addressed independently on its own merits.

chapter III
Proportionate and
Disproportionate Quotas:
The Key Distinction

If Bakke's rights were not violated by the set-aside minority quota used by the University of California at Davis, would any quota have violated his rights? More generally, do quotas ever violate the rights of nonminority individuals? Here, the answer is emphatically yes.

Proportional quotas, because they would naturally occur in a fair world, are not discriminatory at all. While proportional quotas involve the use of race "on its face," which would ordinarily trigger strict scrutiny, they do not discriminate but instead aim to prevent *de facto* racial discrimination from occurring. Their use is a recognition that *ad hoc* measures of merit, however appropriate and innocently motivated, frequently serve to effectuate and validate the society's broader underlying racism. They do not violate the rights of any white individuals "on account of their race" because they do not violate any rights those individuals have, unless they can be said to have the right to profit from society's racism. Thus the use of proportional quotas is compatible with both the spirit and the letter of the Equal Protection Clause—whereas precisely the opposite is true of traditional forms of discrimination. So just as justices are wrong in holding all quotas violative of equal protection, so are they wrong in subjecting quotas to the truly strict scrutiny that the record indicates can never be survived. This is not to say, of course, that benign discrimination should provoke truly relaxed, or "ordinary" judicial scrutiny. Discrimination, properly conceived, *is* discrimination. When a quota is disproportionate it violates the rights of white individuals to their fair shot at society's goods. It violates their rights solely because of their race, which is to say, in a way that is surely offensive to the spirit of the Equal Protection Clause and ought to be held offensive to the letter of it.

The Court majority's current distinction between discrimination against blacks, on the one hand, and whites, on the other—with the latter being acceptable when the goal is the furtherance of an overall fairness to disadvantaged groups—is a dubiously grounded, essentially subjective, and nonneutral principle, and ought to be abandoned. But the Court can do that without employing an insurmountably strict scrutiny against the use of quotas *per se*, as the Court's harshest critics of affirmative action do. If the Court were to keep in mind a vision of nonracist assumptions in a nonracist society, it could save the baby and merely throw out the bathwater. The question would then become not whether the program or policy in question involves the use of race to determine benefits, but whether the allocation of benefits is *unfair* to anyone on the basis of race.

Disproportionate quotas, those which exceed the minority's proportion of the relevant base population, will always be to some degree unfair to nonminority individuals because they impose on a subclass of the majority the burden of "paying back" all that the larger class has taken away. Typically, that larger class includes previous generations. In a fair society, the sons and daughters would be required to forgo the sins of their parents, but they would not be required to pay for those earlier sins by themselves. Nonminority individuals are responsible for minority deficits up to the point of proportionality; their responsibility is to forgo enjoyment of the proportion of benefits they would have lost in fair competition. It is not their responsibility to forgo any of the benefits they would have fairly won—not even if others have been taking more than their share for a long time.

To use the *Bakke* case once again for illustration, suppose that California had attempted to compensate for years of discrimination by admitting only minorities for a given number of years, until the ratio of minority doctors practicing in California matched the ratio of minorities to whites in the general population. Viewed solely in terms of what the minority groups are theoretically entitled to, this would not be unreasonable. The problem is that it would give the minority what the majority owes it, by taking it from only a small percentage of the majority—one narrow age cohort.

Herein lies the only valid meaning of the claim that society may not make its disadvantaged groups whole at the expense of innocent individuals. If we care about fairness, individuals in each generation, each cohort—each relevant population—ought to be allowed to compete for that share of society's benefits which would go to the group under the conditions of racial fairness. Indeed, each individual at each point in life's contest should be allowed to compete for society's benefits under conditions whose odds are those that would prevail under racially fair conditions. To repeat: If society should not reward the children for the sins of their parents, neither should it punish them.

If we believe that race *per se* is no determinant of human potential, and that it is irrelevant to questions of desert, of reward and punishment, then we must conclude that the ideal, completely nonracist society would exhibit racial proportionality in all things. Proportionality would thus be the test of true distributive justice in a society that professed racial equality. In matters of race and equal protection, proportionality would be a touchstone, suggesting where ultimate fairness lies, when rights are truly being infringed on account of race, and when they are only apparently being infringed.[1]

By itself, the proportionality principle can deflect a great many of the objections to affirmative action. Richard Posner, for instance, has asked rhetorically, "Is the position of the whites in this country so unassailable that they cannot be harmed by racial quotas?"[2] Posner's answer, not surprisingly, was that it is not, citing as an "arresting example" of a clearly impermissible preference one offered by John Kaplan. From the premise that "the achievement of political power is one of the fastest ways to equality for an ethnic group," Kaplan had asked, "What then would be wrong with a state's giving Negroes preferential treatment at the ballot box—say, one man, two votes? If the neutral principle that the Constitution is color-blind is unduly simplistic and inappropriate for the complexities of today's world, why is the equally simple principle of one man, one vote entitled to gentler treatment?"[3]

Posner agreed with Kaplan's implicit conclusion that defenders of affirmative action cannot in principle distinguish this proposal from others they find acceptable.[4] But the proposal can easily be distinguished according to the proportionality principle; it is simply a variation of a disproportionate quota. The question of fairness to individuals hinges always on the question of what their benefits—their odds—would be in an ideal society; and in an ideal society, there would be one vote per person, not one for whites and two for minorities.

The proportionality principle is not, of course, a panacea. As I argue below, there are likely to be good-faith disagreements about how proportionality itself should be calculated. In some cases it will be impossible to implement a truly proportional quota. And even where a proportional quota could be implemented, there might be legitimate reasons for not doing so. The innocent persons argument is, after all, only one of many objections to affirmative action; it will still be possible for honorable and intelligent people to object to at least some affirmative action programs, even those that do not violate the rights of innocent persons. When to impose affirmative action will remain a complicated and difficult decision for the society to make.

But when society does choose to impose affirmative action, it ought to employ the proportionality principle. The principle provides a standard for differentiating affirmative action programs that are fair to all individuals from programs that are not. By using it, the society, and the Supreme Court, could ensure that no one is discriminated against on the basis of race.

Formalism

Disproportionate quotas come in many forms, but when they are genuinely disproportionate—as opposed to apparently disproportionate quotas like some of those discussed immediately above—all of them violate individual rights. We have argued that in *Bakke*, Davis would have been justified in implementing something like its set-aside quota. As long as that quota did not exceed the proportion of minorities in the California (or United States) population, Bakke's rights would not have been violated. But if California had attempted to compensate for years of discrimination by admitting only minorities for a given number of years, then the rights of Bakke and all other white would-be applicants during those years would have been violated, since all individuals have a right to compete for their fair share of this important social benefit. So the Supreme Court should strike down such a policy if given the opportunity.

But now suppose that California emphatically wanted to remedy the ills of past discrimination immediately, or at least as soon as possible. Under the principles established here, California would appear to be faced with accepting a gradualist remedy—waiting several decades while the mostly white or all-white graduates of previous years' medical schools were replaced, year by year, with the racially balanced graduating classes of current and future years. Assuming that a physician's professional life averages forty years, it would take that long for California to produce a truly representative body of health-care professionals. In the meantime, California's minorities might continue to receive inadequate or insensitive medical care.

If California were faced with a Supreme Court that had accepted our basic argument, what would its options be, if any? It is not hard to imagine what a determined California legislature might propose: either expand the existing medical schools and create additional minority seats in them or establish additional medical schools devoted entirely to the problem of minority underrepresentation, that is, schools that would accept only minority candidates. Perhaps the legislature might go about this by establishing or greatly expanding a "minority professional scholarship fund" large enough to underwrite the expenses of minority students as well as the added expenses incurred by any existing medical schools that agreed to expand to accommodate the additional students.

It is also not hard to imagine a future "Bakke," a white would-be doctor who applies for one of the "additional" seats in an existing medical school or for one of the seats in an all-new, all-minority medical school. Would she or he be entitled to apply and be seriously considered? On the one hand, it is difficult to argue that she or he is entitled to compete for any of these seats, since they are in fact additional seats—that is, seats created for no other purpose than to increase immediately the number of minority physicians in the state. While the regular seats in the existing medical schools constitute the normal supply of one of society's sought-after privileges, and hence must be made available on a nondiscriminatory, racially fair basis, the additional seats are identifiably and without doubt merely the immediate remedy for a particular social problem. The admission of any white applicants would, of course, be inconsistent with and undermine the legislative goal, which in and of itself must be considered entirely legitimate.

If the Supreme Court were to accept and implement the basic principle outlined here and yet uphold such a program, it would be approving a legislative action consciously designed to circumvent its earlier ruling(s). That is not something the Court likes to—or usually should—do. To do so runs the risk of turning its decisions into hollow forms without practical substance. Yet the Court has frequently done it, typically making the point that the law is frequently indifferent to the legislative motive so long as the ostensible goal is legitimate and the means of achieving the goal are ostensibly reasonable.

There is a better reason for not upholding such a program. The situation undeniably involves the distribution of a social benefit according to a racially disproportionate formula. There, really, is the question: If society may not discriminate in the distribution of existing benefits, may it discriminate in the distribution of newly created benefits? Stated this way, the answer seems obvious. There is nothing about the two cases that would distinguish them on a principled basis. If not one, then not the other, either.

The implication of this is, I think, fairly strong: It would appear to mean that a society may never target a minority for remedial benefits or programs, at least if it involves a racial classification and is either exclusionary or disproportionate. Presumably, programs that are neutral on their face and target a problem that is disproportionately but not uniquely shared by a racial group would be constitutionally acceptable. But state-sponsored allocations of resources to racial groups *as groups* would be forbidden unless they were proportional.

From the standpoint of social policy, this is probably wise. Such programs should normally not be necessary, especially if the basic argument outlined here were taken seriously by the Court. And from the standpoint of constitutional law this is consistent with basic principles. Ordinarily, constitutional rights are assumed to be individual rights which may not be abridged or diluted because the many, acting through the government, wish them to be. The truth is that individual rights are either not properly labeled "rights" or are not taken seriously if they may be taken away from an unconsenting individual by others who share them. This is the case despite arguments to the effect that the Court need not be as suspicious of a majority giving away its own rights as it should be of a majority taking away a minority's rights. Chief Justice Stone's "footnote 4" is the most famous, and perhaps the original, of these latter arguments. In that note to the *Carolene Products Case*[5] the Chief Justice suggested that when majority legislation adversely affects a "discrete and insular minority," the Court will (or should) exercise a stricter scrutiny of it, since the legislation may reflect prejudice and the minority would not be able to use the political processes to obtain a redress of their grievances. By implication, the footnote prescribes a lesser standard of scrutiny for legislation that affects only the majority's exercise of certain rights not specifically protected in the Constitution. It is probably a mistake, however, to take this to mean that less actual constitutional weight should be assigned to these rights. Even though the Chief Justice *was* concerned to rank rights relating to "ordinary commercial transactions" below certain other rights, he was also pointing out that legislatures are simply more likely to pass certain kinds of unconstitutional laws and that the consequences are likely to be more final in some cases than in others if the Court does not strike them down.

It may seem ironic that an argument that relies so heavily on racial calculus should so emphatically disavow any claim of group rights. But nothing here is intended to suggest that group rights are anything more than a sum of individual rights. Reason and statistics tell us what chances an individual should have, what the odds are for an individual in a given endeavor. Those chances, those odds, *are* the individual's rights. The individual has the right, that is, to the odds she or he would have in a fair society. While those odds cannot be calculated without reference to some group, they remain the individual's, as do the rights.

Entitlement

The proportionality principle raises directly the question of individual and group entitlement. Ronald Dworkin has observed that affirmative action programs "seem to encourage . . . a popular misunderstanding, which is that they assume that racial or ethnic groups are entitled to proportionate shares of opportunities, so that

Italian or Polish ethnic minorities are, in theory, as entitled to their proportionate shares as blacks or Chicanos or American Indians are entitled to the shares the present programs give them." But "that is a plain mistake: the programs are not based on the idea that those who are aided are entitled to aid, but only on the strategic hypothesis that helping them is now an effective way of attacking a national problem."[6] This shows that Dworkin's defense of affirmative action is essentially utilitarian. As he subsequently wrote, "I suggest that particular members of minority races have no right to preference, either in reparation for past injustice to others of their own race, or for any other reason. The proper justification of affirmative action programs—if these can be justified at all—lies instead in the benefits such programs might provide for the community as a whole."[7]

Thus, in Dworkin's view, there is no basis for the claims of ethnic groups for "their" share of opportunities because there is no basis for the claims of racial groups—or minority individuals—either. This differs from the position I maintain here on at least one and possibly two counts. The argument here is that individuals do have certain rights, and racial groups have derivative rights, but ethnic groups have neither derivative nor inherent rights.

The argument for proportional quotas rests on a prior claim that individuals have a right to live in a nonracist society or to be treated as they would have been treated in that sort of society. As I indicated earlier, distributive justice, as it relates to race, must be determined by conceiving of the complete eradication of racism, even if that should prove to be a distant or even idle hope in practice. While the right to be free of racism, like all claimed rights, ultimately needs to be justified, it may suffice here to say that the right is one that either is or would be recognized by a wide variety of philosophers, and— more to the point—it seems compatible with Dworkin's own arguments about individual rights. That is, because the right is based on a conception of what all individuals would be entitled to in a fair society, it is a universalizable principle that treats everyone with "equal moral respect"—Dworkin's most basic criterion.[8] It is conceivable and even probable that, his assertion above notwithstanding, Dworkin would accept this claim of individual rights that wind up being "racial rights"—that is, rights individuals have solely because of their race.

It necessarily follows from the right to be free of racism that each individual at each point in life's contest is entitled to compete for society's benefits under conditions whose odds are those that would prevail under racially fair conditions. In turn, that entitlement translates into the right of individual members of every racial group (including whites) to compete for the share of a benefit that the group would have obtained through natural competition in a nonracist society. Thus, the right inevitably and necessarily *makes reference to* the group. But the right remains merely an aggregation of individual rights. It is a mistake to read into the argument here a claim of entitlement by racial groups as such. Rather, what is being advanced is a claim of individual rights that can only be ascertained by reference to the racial group.

There is no claim here for any group *per se*, but only for a kind of derivative claim. It simply turns out that if we are correct about what rights individuals have, and about inherent racial equality, then racial groups will actually receive proportionate shares of society's benefits. And in *one* sense—a rather weak sense—they are entitled to them: because their members are entitled to the opportunities that would produce the collective share. It is true that individual rights are to be determined with reference to the group—it is the group's numbers that determine what odds the individual would have faced in a racially fair world—but whether the group as such thereby possesses any rights depends on further arguments, arguments that need not be (and are not) endorsed here. It is perfectly coherent to maintain that the rights remain the individual's, however they are calculated or aggregated.

What, then, about ethnic groups? Is there not, as Dworkin suggested, a parallel argument available to them? Are not individual members of an ethnic group entitled to certain odds of success which, when aggregated, produce a determinate share for the group? The answer is no, and the reasons are related to the distinctions made above between race and ethnicity.

Let us imagine, for purposes of illustration, an ethnic group that values scholarship disproportionately more than most other groups do, or values and encourages participation in the fine arts, or encourages the entrepreneurial talents of its members. Whatever the distinctive characteristic, let us imagine that the group represents approximately 10 percent of the society. As I noted above, it is possible that the *de facto* "choice" of the group's priorities would be essentially natural—that is, an outgrowth of its own traditions and historical experiences, and essentially undetermined by the prejudices of the larger society. While one cannot discount completely the possibility that stereotyping and subtle discrimination by the larger society have contributed to the perpetuation of any such characteristics—indeed, the argument above suggests that those factors are almost always underestimated—it is nevertheless at least conceivable that a large degree of natural, voluntary ethnic differentiation might have been at work here. (This is most plausible when, as here, the chosen values are ones reasonable people would recognize, even if they might not personally rank them so high.)

To the extent that this is true, or may plausibly be true, then the group may be said to bear at least some responsibility for the relative rates of achievement of its members in relevant fields. That is, if for valid, nondefensive reasons the group *does* "voluntarily" encourage the scholarly achievements of its members, then its members ought not to be limited to 10 percent of the society's scholarly appointments. The group members' disproportionate efforts to rise to the top would have valid, acceptable explanations, and the imposition of proportional quotas would be arbitrary.

The fact that true ethnicity might arguably exist in a fair world means that proportional quotas for ethnic groups cannot be justified by reference to a fair world that levels disparate rates of success and failure for ethnic groups. And by the same token, because ethnic groups might exist in a fair world, they cannot be said to be entitled to any given proportion of society's benefits. That share will depend on the distinctive characteristics of the subculture, which will foster some kinds of achievement and hinder others. It is only because race would not be a determinant of culture in a fair world that it may be discounted as a determinant of relative rates of success and failure in an unfair world.

By extension, ethnic individuals have no claim to any given percentage of society's goods by virtue of their membership in the group. While the degree and kind of "tracking" they have experienced may be said to be accidents of birth beyond their control, the tracking cannot be said to be fundamentally unfair if the larger society, through prejudice, has not encouraged the groups in its deviance from the norm. In one sense, ethnic individuals have the same right that individuals of color have: namely, not to have their chances of success in life affected by the society's prejudice against their group. But once it is accepted that ethnicity may exist in a nonprejudiced world, then it becomes thoroughly problematic to assert that one is owed a given chance of success based on one's membership in an ethnic group of a given size. If it could be shown that the relevant ethnic variation was, in fact, rooted in societal prejudice, and if the contributions of history, language, and the universal need for reference groups could somehow be measured and discounted, then, but only then, could ethnic individuals advance plausible claims of the sorts that racial minorities may advance.

The Supreme Court and the Proportionality Principle

The Supreme Court has occasionally made reference to proportionality, but never to the proportionality principle. It came closest, ironically, in the first case to be decided on the merits. In *Bakke*, four justices raised the possibility that proportionality might be a controlling principle, only to reject it summarily. Relegating the entire argument to a footnote, Justices Brennan, White, Marshall, and Blackmun asserted that "the constitutionality of [the Davis] program is buttressed by its restriction to only 16% of the positions in the Medical School, a percentage less than that of the minority population in California."[9] This less-than-proportional quota was *somehow*

> consistent with the goal of putting minority applicants in the position they would have been in if not for the evil of racial discrimination. Accordingly, this case does not raise the question whether . . . a remedial use of race would be unconstitutional if it admitted . . . as a result of preferential consideration, racial minorities in numbers significantly in excess of their proportional representation in the relevant population. Such programs might well be inadequately justified by the legitimate remedial objectives.[10]

For at least four justices, then, proportional (and/or less-than-proportional) quotas were less objectionable than disproportional quotas for minorities, but the justices provided no explanation of why that should be the case. The suggestion seemed to be that disproportionate quotas were simply too drastic a remedy, or that they were not sufficiently related to "the legitimate remedial objectives"—presumably the ending of discrimination against minorities. Any hope that the plurality took seriously the distinction between proportional and disproportional quotas was immediately put to rest with an emphatic disavowal: "Our allusion to the proportional percentage of minorities in the population of the State administering the program is not intended to establish either that figure or that population universe as a constitutional benchmark."[11] Also suggestive of the justices' ultimate indifference to the proportionality argument is the subsequent claim by one of them that "there is no particular or real significance in the 84–16 division at Davis. The same theoretical, philosophical, social, legal, and constitutional considerations would necessarily apply to the case if Davis' special admissions program had focused on any lesser number."[12] The truth is that both "the proportional percentage of minorities in the population" and the "population universe" are—or should be—"constitutional benchmarks." According to the proportionality argument, there is one, and only one, best quota. A disproportional quota violates the rights of nonminority individuals, and a less-than-proportional quota unfairly rewards nonminority individuals for the society's racism, and in so doing violates the rights of minority individuals to compete for their fair share of society's benefits.

The occasional Court references to proportionality since *Bakke* have similarly never been in a context that would indicate use of the argument here. Thus, for instance, in *Sheet Metal Workers*,[13] Justice Powell noted approvingly that the quota in question was "directly related to the percentage of nonwhites in the relevant workforce."[14] That had been one of four factors the justice had relied on in *Fullilove*,[15] but in neither case was the significance of the factor explained. Justice Powell's simple assertion was quoted approvingly by Justice O'Connor in her dissent in *Paradise*. Arguing that a judicially imposed 50 percent promotion quota was not "narrowly tailored" to the goal of eradicating obstructionism in the Alabama Department of Public Safety when roughly 25 percent of the work force in the lower ranks was black, Justice O'Connor wrote:

> If strict scrutiny is to have any meaning . . . a promotion goal must have a closer relationship to the percentage of blacks eligible for promotions. This is not to say that the percentage of

minority individuals benefitted by a racial goal may never exceed the percentage of minority group members in the relevant work force. But protection of the rights of nonminority workers demands that a racial goal not substantially exceed the percentage of minority group members in the relevant population or work force absent compelling justification.[16]

This passage would appear to be the strongest expression of the relevance of proportionality in any Court opinion, since—unlike the passage in *Bakke*—it contains no disavowal of the general principle. Nonetheless, neither this nor Justice Powell's references to proportionality is an endorsement of the general principle. Not one of these passages makes either of the arguments made here, that in the absence of racism every facet of society would reflect proportionality, and that genuinely proportional quotas (therefore) never violate the rights of individual whites. What these passages do represent, surely, is exactly what the plurality's footnote in *Bakke* represents—an intuitive understanding that *sometimes* proportional quotas represent what would go to minorities under fair conditions. It is surely no coincidence that all of these approving references to proportionality—the latter by justices known as only moderate supporters of affirmative action (at best)[17]—occur in contexts in which the relevant base population is so *obviously* relevant. When admitting students to a state medical school or awarding national contracts or offering membership in a local union or promoting from within an established work force, it doesn't seem to require much speculation to figure what the relevant base population is, and hence what minorities are "entitled" to, that is, what proportion of the benefits in question would naturally go to them.

Any thought that Justice O'Connor's argument was intended to suggest a general principle should be laid to rest by her comment, in the same case, that

[i]n *Sheet Metal Workers*, I observed that "it is completely unrealistic to assume that individuals of each race will gravitate with mathematical exactitude to each employer or union absent unlawful discrimination." Thus, a rigid quota is impermissible because it adopts "an unjustified conclusion about the precise extent to which past discrimination has lingering effects, or . . .

an unjustified prediction about what would happen in the future in the absence of continuing discrimination."[18]

This is as emphatic a *denial* of the general principle of proportionality as one could imagine. Justice O'Connor's implicit, and correct, reasoning is that only by adopting the proportionality principle can one measure the current extent of discrimination and predict what would happen if discrimination were ended. Only if those things can be done, then, can "rigid quotas" be justified. Such quotas are "impermissible" for Justice O'Connor precisely because she believes that neither of the asserted abilities based on the proportionality principle is "justified." The passage supports the view that, far from endorsing a general use of proportionality, Justice O'Connor was not even endorsing its use in that particular case. Her point seems to have been that the quota in question was doubly flawed in being both disproportionate and "rigid"—in effect telling the majority, "even by *your* standards, this quota is unacceptable." This conclusion is bolstered by the fact that both Chief Justice Rehnquist and Justice Scalia—neither of whom has ever indicated support for any affirmative action quota—joined Justice O'Connor's opinion in its entirety and without additional comment.[19]

The failure to adopt the proportionality principle has left the Court without any middle ground on the question of innocence. It has had either to affirm the innocence of white males as a transcendent value over the goals of affirmative action or to denigrate it as a necessary sacrifice. Without the proportionality principle the Court's decisions as a whole have both overstated the extent of white male innocence and undervalued its significance.

It is not surprising that the Court's decisions have been relatively unpersuasive. Most people believe intuitively that there is *something* to the claim of white innocence. Included among them are many who believe that the goals of affirmative action are legitimate and important. Thus, many thoughtful people of goodwill bring strong emotional and intellectual ambivalence to the question. To relieve them of their cognitive dissonance—to help them conquer their ambivalence—the Court's decisions would have to supply a principled middle ground between the competing concerns. But without the proportionality principle to separate valid claims of innocence from invalid ones, the Court has been forced into a series of either-or choices—elevating now one and then the other concern to the primacy of superior principle. In Sullivan's nice characterization, "every time a showdown over the issue has seemed inevitable in the Supreme Court, both sides have been left still standing when the shooting has stopped. Some affirmative action measures have been voted up and some down, but through it all, the Supreme Court has permitted no decisive victory to either side, nor dealt either side a decisive defeat."[20] If our analysis is correct, this is as it should be; no side deserves to triumph fully at the expense of the other. The problem has been that the Court has not supplied good reasons for the partial victories.

Related Constitutional Arguments

Standard of scrutiny. Consistent with its general opposition to affirmative action, the Reagan administration argued that courts should strictly scrutinize *all* race-based laws or policies. Whether of the traditional sort which discriminate against disadvantaged minorities, or of the newer, affirmative action sort which appear to discriminate against nonminorities, they should be struck down unless the government could point to a compelling interest justifying them. This view, shared by other justices, contrasts with the view— a minority position on the Court—that a somewhat lesser standard of review is warranted when the discrimination benefits minorities and penalizes nonminorities. As the administration argued in its brief in the *Paradise* case:[21]

> The proper standard by which to evaluate the constitutionality of race-conscious governmental action under the Equal Protection Clause is now clear. "Racial classifications of any sort must be subjected to 'strict scrutiny.' " *Wygant* . . . (O'Connor, J., concurring in part and concurring in the judgment). Strict scrutiny applies regardless whether the purpose of the discrimination is characterized as malevolent or benign, and regardless of the race of its victims. *E.g., Bakke* . . . (opinion of Powell, J.); *Yick Wo v. Hopkins*. . . . As the plurality stated in *Wygant*, "the level of scrutiny does not change merely because the challenged classification operates against a group that historically has not been subjected to governmental discrimination. . . ."

> Any less stringent analysis, such as a "test of 'reasonableness,'"
> ... has no support in the decisions of this Court.[22]

Along with the four plurality justices in *Wygant*, the administration's *Paradise* brief counted Justice White as a fifth justice insisting on strict scrutiny even in benign discrimination cases. As proof the administration cited the fact that Justice White had joined that portion of Justice Powell's opinion in *Bakke* which said, "Racial and ethnic distinctions of any sort are inherently suspect and thus call for the most exacting judicial examination."[23] The administration also pointed to Justice Stevens's dissent in *Fullilove v. Klutznick*[24] as evidence that he too subscribes to this view, although it acknowledged that his dissent in *Wygant* rendered his position ambiguous.

The administration counted three justices as expressing "the view that a somewhat less rigorous standard is appropriate where a racial classification discriminates against white persons. See, *e.g.*, *Wygant* . . . (Marshall, J., joined by Brennan and Blackmun, JJ., dissenting). These Justices nevertheless have required a '"strict and searching" . . . inquiry' in such instances."[25] Thus, by the administration's count, five justices during the 1987 term essentially held to the view that discrimination is discrimination and must always be subjected to strict scrutiny, while three justices held the contrary view and one justice was uncertain.

A more accurate accounting would probably acknowledge that Justices Powell and Stevens tended to pay lip service to the single standard while being considerably more receptive to benign discrimination than to traditional discrimination. In *Paradise*, for instance, the two voted to uphold the district court's quota—a disproportionate quota at that. In addition, many observers have noted that Justice Powell's rather famous opinion in *Bakke* claiming to employ strict scrutiny wasn't really persuasive. Having insisted that the Davis admissions plan would have to withstand strict scrutiny and could be upheld only if a "compelling interest" were found to justify it, the justice proceeded to find in "academic freedom" just that compelling interest. Many have wondered whether Justice Powell would have found "academic freedom" compelling enough if a state school had discriminated *against* minorities. Virtually every other opinion by him in race cases indicates that he would not have. Thus, on the 1987 Court there were probably five justices who were at least somewhat more receptive to discrimination against nonminorities than they were to discrimination against minorities, and four justices who were apparently equally disposed against both.

Quotas and race as a suspect category. Closely related to the standard-of-scrutiny discussion is the argument that any quotas, even proportional ones, would violate the Equal Protection Clause simply because they employ the suspect classification of race, a practice which in and of itself is forbidden. This is a common argument among critics of affirmative action, and the Supreme Court has occasionally suggested this line of reasoning. It did so, for example, when it struck down antimiscegenation laws in *Loving v. Virginia*.[26] In that case the state had argued that because the statute punished both the white and the black party in an interracial marriage, there was no *discrimination* on the basis of race involved, and hence no violation of the Equal Protection Clause. Speaking for a unanimous Court, Chief Justice Warren wrote: "[Here], we deal with statutes containing racial classifications, and the fact of equal application does not immunize the statute from the very heavy burden of justification which the Fourteenth Amendment has traditionally required of state statutes drawn according to race."[27]

The conclusion sometimes drawn from cases like *Loving* is that the Fourteenth Amendment mandates color-blind laws, and that the mere *use* of racial categories by the government is forbidden, or at least highly suspect. Thus, even if it were granted that proportional quotas are not *unfair* to white individuals, they would be forbidden simply because they employ racial classifications; they are racist on their face.

The truth, however, is that the well-earned modern suspicion of racial classifications is just that—a suspicion, not an absolute and independent constitutional principle. It is twice grounded: in the extreme historical correlation between racial classifications and invidious discrimination, which it was the purpose of the Fourteenth Amendment to overcome, and in the belief that racial classifications are "in most circumstances irrelevant to any constitutionally acceptable legislative purpose."[28] The Court knows that when a classification is irrelevant to the stated goal, the law is either arbitrary or invidious or both.

While the suspicion rightly generates strict scrutiny, it follows that the suspicion can be overcome by a twofold showing that the discrimination is not invidious and that the classification is relevant to an acceptable purpose. A careful reading of even the *Loving* decision supports this view:

> [The] clear and central purpose of the Fourteenth Amendment was to eliminate all official state sources of invidious racial discrimination in the States. . . . [At] the very least, the Equal Protection Clause demands that racial classifications, especially suspect in criminal statutes, be subjected to the "most rigid scrutiny," and, if they are ever to be upheld, they must be shown to be necessary to the accomplishment of some permissible state objective, independent of the racial discrimination which it was the object of the Fourteenth Amendment to eliminate.[29]

Loving and cases like it[30] were concerned with laws aimed at keeping the races apart. Those laws were designed to, and to some degree did, maintain the overall system of white supremacy in the southern states where they existed. It was clearly error to read evenhanded enlightenment into the fact that they punished offending whites and blacks equally. A glimpse below the surface shows incontestably that complete enforcement and punishment were integral parts of an invidious system: if it took two parties to undermine white supremacy, it simply made sense to hard-core racists to deter both parties. It was entirely appropriate for the Court to look at the context of the laws and to judge them thoroughly invidious under the traditional purposes of the Fourteenth Amendment and without relevance to any permissible purpose.

By contrast, even critics of affirmative action do not assert that quotas are designed to harm minorities. And whatever one thinks of the wisdom or the efficacy of racial quotas, no one can deny that they are *relevant* to the "constitutionally acceptable legislative purpose" of counteracting the effects of racial discrimination. Here, they are clearly not mere subterfuges for prejudice but are in fact the single most obviously efficient means to the goal. Because critics can and do argue that affirmative action quotas may wind up hurting minorities—simply because they *do* employ explicit racial classifications—the Court should continue to hold their use up to heightened scrutiny and to judge whether they are in fact "necessary to the accomplishment of some permissible state objective." If our analysis is correct, the Court should also ask whether the quotas treat any individuals unfairly because of their race—that is, whether the quota is disproportionate. But the stated criteria suggest that even the *Loving* Court would have distinguished affirmative action from invidious uses of racial classification—especially when no one was being treated unfairly on account of race.

When no one is being treated unfairly, the use of racial classifications loses its most potent constitutional objection. Unlike the Court majority's current distinction between discrimination against whites, on the one hand, and discrimination against blacks, on the other, there is a set of neutral principles to be had here: no use of race except to *avoid discrimination*, and *no actual discrimination*. In short, if all that is left of purely constitutional arguments against quotas is the formalistic requirement of facial neutrality, then there is not much left. The argument against "reverse discrimination" was always strongest when it emphasized that actual discrimination was occurring. To the degree that the proportionality argument addresses that argument, all that remains of purely constitutional objections to affirmative action quotas *per se* is that easily rebuttable formalism.

The proportionality principle and de facto *discrimination.* There remain two points of constitutional interest to be addressed. The first relates to the fact that the Equal Protection Clause is directed at state action. Purely private acts of discrimination are not covered by it. Yet the proportionality argument makes less use of official discrimination than of such "private" discrimination—*i.e.*, the virtually infinite number of racially conscious acts by individuals which in their aggregate produce race-correlated disparities in the society. The argument holds that without these countless acts of mostly private, mostly low-level racism, blacks and whites would succeed and fail in equal measure in all things. Thus, the lack of proportionality in any given situation is taken as proof of essentially private discrimination.

This means that courts cannot use the Equal Protection Clause by itself to remedy such discrimination. Thus, no federal court can invoke the clause as the source of proportional quotas, for that would be to apply it to essentially *de facto* rather than *de jure* discrimination. Even when one of the parties in a case is a state agency, the proportionality argument cannot be used to support a Fourteenth Amendment *requirement* of proportionality—a judicial order imposing a proportional quota as a remedy—because the state agency will arguably not have contributed to the lack of proportionality.

This important point is less of an obstacle to judicial employment of the proportionality principle than it seems, however. As most students of constitutional law know, Congress has the authority to regulate private acts of discrimination under its power to regulate interstate commerce. Since Congress passed the 1964 Civil Rights Act under the authority of the Commerce Clause, the only question for the Court has been whether its various provisions—especially Titles VI (education) and VII (employment)—require, or even permit, either the voluntary use of quotas or their imposition by federal judges.

My own reading of the legislative debate convinces me that the primary political actors either were not aware of the proportionality argument or rejected it. While the bill's sponsors explicitly endorsed the goal of eliminating the effects of societal discrimination in employment and education, they also explicitly, if perhaps defensively and unthinkingly, rejected the conclusion that a lack of discrimination would necessarily produce proportional representation, and for that and other reasons rather strongly disavowed the use of quotas to end discrimination.[31] Even by the most expansive reading of Title VII, Section 703(j), Congress intended to relieve employers of the need to take proportionality into account in meeting their obligations not to discriminate.[32] A justice who wishes to be faithful to congressional intent and yet believes in the proportionality argument would thus have to choose between the legislators' "erroneous" particular belief and their broader goal—a not unfamiliar dilemma.

A sharply divided Court has interpreted these statutes to permit federal judges to impose quotas to *correct* particularly "egregious" or "persistent" prior discrimination, and to *permit* voluntary use of at least "moderate, flexible, case-by-case" programs of preferential treatment in most other cases. The preceding statutory interpretations notwithstanding, this is not as unwarranted as it might seem. As Fallon and Weiler noted, "the general *remedial* provision of Title

VII is entirely open textured in its authorization to the federal courts to order such relief as they may deem appropriate, and the courts of appeals are unanimous in finding there a warrant for remedial quotas."[33] The Supreme Court has not been so unanimous: the liberal plurality in *Sheet Metal Workers* held that Section 703(j) does not prohibit federal courts from imposing these proportional quotas as a remedy for proven, past discrimination, but the proposition was sharply challenged by Justice O'Connor.[34]

If no further congressional action is taken, the Court can use the proportionality argument to *uphold* proportional quotas in most cases of private discrimination, and to *impose* them itself in others—although it must be said that its authority could be less ambiguously given in new legislation. When a case involves the Fourteenth Amendment rather than Title VI or VII, the proportionality argument can and should still play a critical role. In defeating the argument that white males are being unfairly discriminated against, the proportionality argument can allow the amendment to be used to *uphold a state-imposed quota* like the one in *Bakke*. It simply can't be used to impose one itself, unless it expands the Thirteenth Amendment. Otherwise, given current and widely accepted interpretations of the Fourteenth Amendment, only Congress, using its commerce power, can give the federal courts the power to do that.

Scholarly Comment and the Proportionality Principle: Ronald Dworkin and the Rights of Whites

Scholarly commentators have been less reluctant to award victory to one side or the other. With few exceptions they have urged the Court to award a decisive victory to their chosen side and a decisive defeat to the other. Although her analysis is more sophisticated than most, Sullivan is in this respect, at least, typical. The Court's problem, in her analysis, is not that it lacks a principled way to stay in the middle but that it has allowed itself to be trapped there by using a "sin-based paradigm" of affirmative action. It has approved affirmative action

> only as precise penance for the specific sins of racism a government, union, or employer has committed in the past. . . . Not surprisingly, this approach has invited claims . . . that non-

sinners—white workers "innocent" of their bosses' or union leadership's past discrimination—should not pay for "the sins of others of their own race," nor should nonvictims benefit from their sacrifice.[35]

By focusing on sin, that is, the paradigm actually *invites* claims of innocence. The Court has thus unwittingly cultivated ambivalence. By conceiving affirmative action in such a way that it thrusts claims of innocence (and undeserved advantage) to the fore, it has exacerbated the tension unnecessarily:

> Trapped in the paradigm of sin, the Court shrinks, even in upholding affirmative action plans, from declaring that the benefits of building a racially integrated society for the future can be justification enough. . . . And hemmed in by the quandary of harm to innocents that a sin-based rationale inevitably creates, the Court continues to caution, even in upholding affirmative action, that it is but a necessary evil. Not surprisingly, affirmative action's proponents and opponents both find reason to triumph: its proponents in the declaration of its necessity; its opponents, in its definition as evil.[36]

The clear implication of Sullivan's analysis is that the claims of white innocence are, in fact, less valid than they are made to appear, if they are valid at all.[37] Having observed that the Court has never successfully answered the twin objections of white innocence and undeserving minority beneficiaries "from within a sin-based paradigm," Sullivan suggested that "it might have either by viewing the category of black 'victims' of past discrimination expansively, or by discounting claims of white 'innocence.'"[38] That is, the Court should have considered "expanding the concepts of white sin or black injury"[39] in order to effectively rebut the claims of individual white innocence and undeserved benefits by individual blacks.

Since it was not her preferred approach to stay within the sin-based paradigm, Sullivan did not elaborate these suggestions, but it seems reasonably clear that the suggestion is for the Court to employ a group-based theory of guilt and desert. As I argued earlier, however, that tactic would necessarily involve the Court in an inherently racist assignment of rights and duties. Crudely put, it amounts to this: If you were born white, you share your white ancestors' crimes; if you were born black, you are entitled to share in what was owed to your black ancestors or your contemporary brothers and sisters. It is not an approach likely to diminish good-faith objections to affirmative action.[40]

Sullivan's preferred resolution of the Court's dilemma is to escape the sin-based paradigm entirely, and instead to develop a forward-looking paradigm rather than one that looks back, one which justifies affirmative action as "the architecture of a racially integrated future."[41] Sullivan thinks the Court may have avoided forward-looking justifications because they would open it to "charges that, by seeking the result of increased minority representation, [affirmative action] plans are a dangerous exercise in 'social engineering.' "[42] But she clearly thinks the advantages outweigh the risks.

Given the unsatisfactory nature of the Court's current approach, that may be a correct judgment. But our concern here is with the implication that a forward-looking justification would truly nullify concerns about white innocence rather than simply camouflage or finesse them. Even if we grant that a forward-looking justification of affirmative action is more compelling than one based on the righting of particular wrongs, it does not follow that the claims of white innocence are then worth nothing, or that they disappear from the equation. Without a persuasive argument that the claims of whites are inherently invalid, honesty would require acknowledging that the rights of innocent whites are still being sacrificed for the greater (future) good, even if not so blatantly.

Sullivan's position here appears to be that in the new paradigm the sacrifice is more appropriate, or rather less inappropriate:

If . . . aspirations for the future rather than past sin were the basis for affirmative action, would white claims of "innocence" count for less? They should, for it is easier to show that displacing "innocent" whites is narrowly tailored to goals that turn on integrating institutions now than it is to show that doing so is narrowly tailored to purging past sins of discrimination that the displaced whites did not themselves "commit."[43]

It is Sullivan's great insight that if one removes the punishment-reward justification, the claim of innocence tends to become irrelevant. In the proposed paradigm the society is in effect saying, "We, the dominant majority, are simply going to institute a policy that will make us a better society, and as with all policies, someone has to pay. Forget about who is to blame for the problem; it doesn't matter. How the costs of the policy are distributed is in no way related to relative guilt or innocence. Politics is often unfair in that sense."

Whatever Sullivan's own views on individual white innocence may be, it appears that in the new paradigm one need have no quarrel with the claim. The logic of her position is that the innocence is irrelevant, so there is no longer a need to deny that at least some whites are innocent of causing harm to blacks. Moreover, there is no need (and in Sullivan's passages there is no attempt) to deny that some of them will be the ones called on to make sacrifices, because in the new paradigm their sacrifices are reduced to an ordinary sort in no need of special—i.e., constitutional—justification. There is substantial power in this implicit argument that the achievement of the common good frequently requires uneven sacrifices by citizens, so it must be granted that Sullivan's proposed justification of affirmative action is indeed less vulnerable in its own terms than the Court's "sin-based" justifications are.

If there is a problem here, it can only be because race is involved. If the logic of affirmative action somehow made it appropriate to place most of the burden on the rich or the poor, or on midwesterners or rural people or smart or thin people, it seems clear that the issue could properly be left to politics. But because the logic of affirmative action requires that certain *whites* bear the burden, there is arguably a greater need to justify imposing the burden. The Fourteenth Amendment, after all, forbids politics to be unfair in certain ways.

Thus, whether Sullivan's proposed change of paradigms really avoids the problems of *unconstitutional* unfairness to sometimes innocent whites depends on the question of whether they have any special claim beyond those of numerous other political actors—whether, that is, there is something special, and forbidden, about imposing burdens on the basis of being white in a given situation.

That there is not something special is mostly implicit in Sullivan's analysis. But Ronald Dworkin has explicitly argued that discrimination against whites stands on a lower constitutional plane than discrimination against blacks. In separate articles Professor Dworkin has argued that neither Marco DeFunis nor Allan Bakke "had a case,"[44] even though it is implicit that they were innocent of any personal discrimination against minorities.

In discussing the then-pending *Bakke* case, Dworkin initially seemed to suggest that the compelling interest in a racially equal society simply outweighs the claims of individual whites to fair treatment: "The history of the campaign against racial injustice since 1954 . . . is a history in large part of failure. We have not succeeded in reforming the racial consciousness of our society by racially neutral means. We are therefore obliged to look upon the arguments for affirmative action with sympathy and an open mind."[45] But Dworkin subsequently disclaimed this easy route: "It may be argued that even if the programs *are* effective in making our society less a society dominated by race, they are nevertheless unconstitutional because they violate the individual constitutional rights of those, like Allan Bakke, who lose places in consequence."[46] And: "Of course, if Bakke is right that such programs, no matter how effective they may be, violate his constitutional rights then they cannot be permitted to continue."[47]

So everything depends on how Bakke's rights are characterized. And Bakke's individual rights, in Dworkin's view, are determined by whether the society was motivated by prejudice toward Bakke's group. The various "slogans" thought to identify a constitutional right for Bakke "can stand for no genuine principle except one. This is the important principle that no one in our society should suffer because he is a member of a group thought less worthy of respect, as a group, than other groups."[48] Bakke's claim "not to be excluded from medical school because of his race alone" merely "sounds plausible" because "it suggests the following more complex principle. Every citizen has a constitutional right that he not suffer disadvantage, at least in the competition for any public benefit, because the race or religion or sect or region or other natural or artificial group to which he belongs is the object of prejudice or contempt."[49] And:

> The popular argument frequently made on editorial pages is that Bakke has a right to be judged on his merit. Or that he has a right to be judged as an individual rather than as a member of a social group. Or that he has a right, as much as any black man, not to be sacrificed or excluded from an opportunity because

of his race alone. But these catch phrases are deceptive here, because, as reflection demonstrates, the only genuine principle they describe is the principle that no one should suffer from the prejudice or contempt of others.[50]

Dworkin's constitutional argument thus reduces to the now-familiar one that racial discrimination is only unconstitutional if it is invidious—that is, motivated by prejudice. Leaving aside for a moment the claim that the individual's rights do not extend beyond the right not to be victimized by society's invidious attitudes toward the group, this tends to be tautological as a defense of affirmative action: benign discrimination is different from invidious discrimination because it isn't invidious. But it is based on a reading of the Equal Protection Clause as prohibiting one and not the other, so its validity depends on the validity of that reading. And there is, in fact, substantial merit to the view that, with regard to race, the clause almost certainly was aimed at the effects of racial prejudice and was therefore not intended to make race a wholly impermissible legal classification—was not, that is, intended to prohibit so-called benign discrimination, discrimination designed to counteract the effects of prejudice.

Dworkin was not content to let the matter lie with a simple recitation of constitutional history. The underlying reason why discrimination against whites is acceptable while discrimination against blacks is not is that the former may be relevant to the achievement of a constitutionally legitimate and important social goal whereas the latter can never be. Thus, while there may be an individual right not to be discriminated against "for irrelevant reasons,"

> . . . race is not irrelevant when an important social goal is to reduce racial consciousness. . . . [W]hat is relevant, in deciding whom to train to become a doctor, depends upon fact, not convention. If a certain form of treatment requiring physically strong doctors became popular, then physical strength, not now relevant, would become so. It is regrettable that the facts now make race relevant, but they do.[51]

To rebut the charge that the same argument could be applied to discrimination against minorities, Dworkin again invoked the special purposes of the Equal Protection Clause. Whereas it is compatible with the purposes of the clause to pursue overall racial fairness, even by extending special aid to disadvantaged minorities, it can never be a legitimate state purpose to further disadvantage them, to perpetuate the advantages of the traditionally favored racial majority.

Thus, while agreeing that whites have the same theoretical rights as blacks, Dworkin concluded that there are two reasons why the former may be discriminated against on the basis of race while the latter may not. In the first place, there is no special constitutional prohibition of discrimination against generally favored racial majorities, but only against generally disfavored racial minorities; and in the second place, discrimination against members of the favored majority may be relevant to the achievement of an important and constitutionally acceptable goal, as it can never be in the case of disfavored-minority individuals.

Although many have found Dworkin's argument unpersuasive,[52] that fact may say more about the many-faceted nature of the question than about the argument as such. As a purely constitutional argument, it is at least entirely coherent, relying as it does on the familiar criteria of historical intent and spirit. Those criteria are in themselves neutral even if Dworkin used them to reach "non-neutral" results. That use does not seem to me essentially contrived or obviously flawed; in this case, at least, the intent and spirit seem fairly clear.

Nonetheless, is it so clear that "exclusion on irrelevant grounds violates a person's rights only in those cases involving contempt or prejudice for a group"?[53] After all, as one of Dworkin's critics has observed:

> Surely it is at least as much a concern that the value and dignity of individuals be protected, and this value and dignity is undercut by practices such as exclusion from public benefits by irrelevant tests such as race (or religion, or sex, or sexual preferences). And just as surely, an individual's worth and dignity can be threatened by such tests in individual cases, irrespective of their impact on groups. . . . Bakke does have a right to be judged on his own merits even though, should he not be so judged, he will not suffer from contempt or prejudice.[54]

Dworkin's response that "race is not irrelevant" in affirmative action cases reflects his focus on the rights of whites as a group under the Equal Protection Clause rather than on the rights of individuals to fairness generally. Dworkin and his critics have to some extent been speaking past each other because of a failure to appreciate the sense in which race is relevant in affirmative action cases on the macro, or societal, level but not on the micro, or individual, level. That is, there can be no denying that when it comes to remedies for racial discrimination, race is supremely relevant. At the same time, Dworkin cannot really deny that when it comes to an individual applying to medical school (or law or business school, or white- or blue-collar jobs, *etc.*, *etc.*), race *per se* is an inherently irrelevant factor. It becomes relevant only when one adds the racially explicit societal goal to the consideration. It is thus somewhat circular to say that race is relevant in affirmative action cases; it is relevant only because, and to the extent that, the goals of affirmative action have made it so. What remains is the sense of unfairness that factors acknowledged by all to be extraneous to the real questions of merit and desert have been admitted into consideration.

It may well be that the Equal Protection Clause was designed to prohibit discrimination originating in prejudice. It may also be that, for reasons of political wisdom or constitutional fidelity or both, the clause should be read as tolerating discrimination relevant to the achievement of overall racial fairness. But even if all this were to be granted, it would remain true that the imposition of a disproportionate quota would require innocent whites to sacrifice more than they should have to—more than they would in a fair world. In the views of both Dworkin and Sullivan, this sacrifice is denied constitutional stature, but it is not thereby obliterated. It is reduced to the status of countless other unfair sacrifices imposed by the game of politics. Dworkin compared Bakke's and DeFunis's rejections to rejection on the basis of intelligence or to rejection in favor of an otherwise equally qualified veteran—the point being that the choice of admissions criteria is essentially up to the institutions in question as long as they are plausibly related to the common good:

> Any admissions policy must put some applicants at a disadvantage, and a policy of preference for minority applicants can reasonably be supposed to benefit the community as a whole,

even when the loss to candidates such as DeFunis is taken into account. . . . The disadvantage to applicants such as DeFunis is . . . a cost that must be paid for a greater gain; it is in that way like the disadvantage to less intelligent students that is the cost of ordinary admissions policies.[55]

But racial politics is never just like any other politics; nor should it be. Race clearly ought to remain a suspect classification in politics as well as law. That is at least as much the real point of the Equal Protection Clause as the prohibition of discrimination based on group prejudice. If, as articles like those of Sullivan and Dworkin argue, race should not be so suspect that benign goals cannot be pursued, neither should it be considered so tolerable that we undermine the idea that race *per se* is never relevant to any legitimate social goal. If, in those very few cases where it is arguably relevant—the list may well start and end with affirmative action—we allow individuals to be discriminated against on account of their race, we risk not so much setting a dangerous precedent as engendering cynicism about equal protection itself.

We ought, somehow, to seek a way of accommodating affirmative action that does not undermine the hard-won and critically protective principle that race is irrelevant. We ought to embrace any approach that promises to avoid discrimination against whites simply because they are white. The proportionality principle will surely not be accepted by many people, at least as a practical guide for actual cases. But to the extent that it is coherent, it gives just that promise. At the same time that it intends to demolish the usual claims of whites not to have to sacrifice anything, it promises to protect them against excessive sacrifices, sacrifices unfairly imposed simply because of race.

Interestingly enough, Dworkin unintentionally provided an analogy that might be useful here. To illustrate his point that when directed against whites, at least, racial discrimination is no special deal, Dworkin pointed out:

There is nothing paradoxical . . . in the idea that an individual's right to equal protection may sometimes conflict with an otherwise desirable social policy, including the policy of making the community more equal overall. Suppose a law school were to charge a few middle-class students, selected by lot, double tuition in order to increase the scholarship fund for poor students. It would be serving a desirable policy—equality of opportunity—by means that violated the right of the students selected by lot to be treated equally with other students who could also afford the increased fees.[56]

The point is that while the policy may not be *fair*, it is acceptable because it furthers a "desirable social policy," and we are to understand that such occurrences are so common as to be the rule rather than the exception. But Dworkin did see an objection here. The policy is *unnecessarily* unfair to the students selected at random and charged double fees: "The special disadvantage to these students was not necessary to achieve the gain in scholarship funds, because the same gain would have been achieved by a more equal distribution of the cost amongst all the students who could afford it."[57]

Here Dworkin implicitly identified the broadest meaning of the Equal Protection Clause, which is that discrimination on irrelevant grounds should be avoided if there are other ways of achieving a legitimate social purpose. This principle of equal protection is even more basic than the principle that discrimination based on prejudice should be avoided. It argues against imposing social costs in an unfair or irrational way; it argues that those costs ought to be equally borne by all who are equally situated with regard to the policy in question. The fact that Dworkin's invocation of the principle is left unexplained is, in fact, testimony to how well established it is (even if it is often violated to some extent by governments of all sorts, and even if the Supreme Court passes over it in cases involving regulation of ordinary commercial transactions). Laws or policies that impose costs disproportionately or without reason violate the essential rationality of law—the inherent rationality that makes law law—that has been a component of traditional due process for hundreds of years and which informed the very idea of equal protection, namely, that those equally situated should be treated equally.

By analogy, the problem with unbounded affirmative action—which does not acknowledge the proportionality argument—is that it may sometimes impose the costs of a worthwhile social policy on too few people. It may extract the costs disproportionately from a subset of the people who should be bearing the costs.

At a minimum, as even Dworkin acknowledged, such a policy is flawed; it is undeniably unfair. And if the unfairness in even Dworkin's example rises to somewhere near the level of constitutional objection, then how much more obviously does race-based unfairness approach it? It may well be that Dworkin has identified the true intent, or the true spirit, of the Equal Protection Clause as it regards racial minorities; and if only by contrast, one would think, that intent and spirit ought to cover the rights of nonminorities. But when that intent, that spirit, collides with a prior, even more basic spirit of equal protection, and when even the spirit of racial fairness is jeopardized by a policy of ignoring the more basic spirit, then it is not farfetched to conclude that *all* racial unfairness must be avoided.

Although Dworkin's interpretation of the Equal Protection Clause is ultimately literalist in the sense that it fastens on the particular historical intent of the framers rather than on the truly universal principles of law or political philosophy that underlie all broad constitutional provisions, his use of the clause correctly rejects the simplistic, literalist interpretation of it in favor of one that goes to the historically actual spirit of it. The problem, however, is that Dworkin's interpretation doesn't go far enough in identifying the most basic principle informing equal protection. Dworkin might ask why the framers of the Fourteenth Amendment wished to prohibit discrimination based on prejudice. And the answer is not simply that prejudice had produced slavery and would produce something like it again if not controlled, although that is the actual historical problem the framers had in mind. The more basic answer is that discrimination based on prejudice is irrational. Virtually by definition, prejudice involves false assumptions about people—more particularly, about a characteristic shared by them—and the falseness of the assumptions leads to treating people differently. The prohibition against racial discrimination makes no sense unless it is coupled with the framers' belief—or, at least, public affirmation—that race was no fit basis for distinguishing among people. That, in turn, was based on an assumption of racial equality, an assumption that discrimination on the basis of race was unjust and irrational, slavery and second-class citizenship based on race were unjust and irrational, and racial prejudice was to be discouraged because it produced unfairness.

In one form or another, Dworkin's argument has reappeared in later commentaries, even the most sophisticated. For example, Sullivan has argued that whites are actually not being discriminated against on the basis of their race at all, and hence are not being victimized in the first place: "as long as whites displaced by affirmative action are not being subordinated on the basis of their race—as it is especially clear they are not when white-dominated governments, unions, or employers *choose* affirmative action—any important purpose for affirmative action should be justification enough."[58]

Most other commentators have implicitly or explicitly accepted the innocent persons argument. Lacking the proportionality principle, they have faced the same unsatisfactory choices the Court has faced. And like the Court's decisions, they have failed to present arguments that are wholly convincing. Once one has accepted the general innocence of white males, justifying affirmative action becomes highly problematic. It is not surprising, therefore, that the most interesting of the countless commentaries are those which seem to accept the innocence of white males yet seek to justify the use of affirmative action programs that sacrifice their interests.

chapter IV
Applying the Principles:
The Supreme Court and
Affirmative Action

In General

If our argument to this point is sound, the Supreme Court and its critics have overlooked a controlling principle that ought to guide its affirmative action decisions. If the principle were to be adopted by the Court, it would resolve, or at least greatly clarify, a major debate within the larger controversy. If, when the Court is asked to judge an affirmative action program it were to employ the test of proportionality, it would ensure fairness to white individuals. When that test is properly used, there is no violation of anyone's rights—no taking of anything that anyone had a right to expect or claim—because proportional quotas treat everyone precisely as they would be treated if race *were* completely irrelevant, completely ignored. Hence their use cannot constitute discrimination against anyone on the basis of race. Indeed, far from violating the command of the Equal Protection Clause not to discriminate on the basis of race, the use of proportional quotas in any given situation helps prevent societal discrimination from culminating in one of its many unjust final disparities.

Almost as important as the fact of nondiscrimination is the avoidance of the apparent need to justify discrimination. If white individuals are not being unfairly discriminated against on the basis of race, then supporters of affirmative action do not have to argue for the dubious, nonneutral principle that the Equal Protection Clause permits such discrimination when the goal is legitimate and socially important. And, conversely, critics of affirmative action would not be able to argue that "discrimination is discrimination," that the clause forbids treating *any individual*—white as well as black—unfairly solely because of his or her race. Supporters of affirmative action could respond that when proportional quotas are used, *nobody* is being treated unfairly.

But a caution is probably in order. The argument at the heart of this book should not be read as necessarily endorsing the use of proportional quotas whenever and wherever a racial disparity occurs. Rather, the argument aims to remove one critical constitutional objection to their use. It is intended to show that there is often no discrimination against the innocent white individuals involved, and hence no constitutional violation of equal protection. The appropriate conclusion is that the Equal Protection Clause poses no *barrier* to the use of quotas. But this is not the same as endorsing their widespread use. Surely there are other arguments the society has a right to consider.

In the first place, the application of proportional quotas will necessarily involve explicitly race-conscious calculations. Determining what an individual's rights are and whether they have been violated will require determining what that individual's odds of attaining a given benefit would be in the ideal state. That means determining, in each situation, which relevant demographic group the individual represents and what the overall racial distribution of benefits would be in that ideal state. These determinations will inevitably be distasteful, to say the least, to people who have been taught to abjure racial thinking. It surely seems a step backward, if our goal is to produce a nonracist society, to encourage thinking of individual rights in terms of the racial group to which the individual belongs.

More important, a rigid and thorough enforcement of the proportionality principle raises the possibility of unwittingly stigmatizing minorities, and of unwittingly exacerbating race consciousness and racial antagonism in the society. While the aphorism that the remedy for racism will sometimes require thinking in racial terms is a reasonable response here, as is the exhortation to be unflinching in pursuit of racial justice, so are the responses of caution and *ad hoc* judgment. Society ought, probably, to be allowed to judge when proportional quotas are called for and when their employment would do more harm than good, and the Court should simply acquiesce in that judgment.

Fortunately, this comports with a widely accepted view of the Court's current constitutional and statutory authority. Since most of the racial disparities to be corrected are the result of innumerable subtle acts of *de facto* discrimination rather than *de jure* discrimination, the Equal Protection Clause cannot properly be used to impose quotas generally. Rather, it can be used only passively, as it were, to uphold the imposition of quotas by the states and their political subdivisions. If there is to be federal judicial authority for imposing quotas generally, it must come from Congress, expressing the wishes of the society to finally eradicate the widespread effects of systemic discrimination.

Because, in my view, the grant of that authority in the 1964 Civil Rights Act is ambiguous, I would hold more or less to the course apparently chosen by the Court in the last two terms. Approving the voluntary use of quotas by employers (and universities, *etc.*) where the calculation of proportionality is relatively unproblematic, and upholding the power of federal courts to order the imposition of such quotas when there has been a showing of "egregious" or "persistent" discrimination by the party in question—but also unequivocally upholding the authority of states to impose proportional quotas—seems to me a reasonable accommodation of constitutional, statutory, and political authority.

In any case, even if the Court were to adopt the essential arguments here, it would face difficulties which themselves argue for restraint. If the proportionality principle is clear enough as a principle, its application will be problematic in many cases. Problems will arise for courts calculating proportionality when it is unclear what "group" the nonminority individual belongs to in the particular situation—that is, what the relevant cohort is—and what the relevant base population or "population universe" is. Until both are established, the proportional quota cannot be calculated.

Local versus National Standards

A court willing to employ the proportionality principle will first have to decide whether to impose essentially local standards or a national standard. That decision will implicate theoretical assumptions and will reflect the degree to which the judge adheres to the core arguments here. Even apparently simple cases will often present this choice. Thus, for instance, the Bakke case at first appears to be straightforward enough: When an affirmative action program involves admissions decisions, it seems clear that each entering class will usually constitute the relevant cohort because the vast majority of applicants fall into a narrow range of ages (Bakke himself notwithstanding); the proportion of seats to be allotted would be the same as the proportion of the races for those age brackets in the general population. In those less frequent cases in which the pool of applicants is cross-generational, the relevant cohort will either be the same as the base population—that is, the entire population—or it will be weighted to reflect the age brackets represented in the applicant pool.

When the school in question is a state school that draws applicants essentially from within the state (as in Bakke), the relevant base population would seem to be the entire population of the state. In such cases an individual white applicant would, under fair conditions, compete with an applicant pool reflecting the racial composition of the state generally, and thus would be entitled, in an imperfect world, to compete for the share of seats equal to the proportion of whites within the state. If the applicant pool is drawn from outside as well as inside the state, then the base population of those areas would have to be factored in and given proportional weight.

These calculations will be complex but manageable. It might seem that they pose questions so complex and problematical that, to use the Court's language in Baker v. Carr, they have no "judicially discoverable and manageable standards." They might seem, that is, to place the whole matter into the "political questions" category. But there is a relatively simple answer to this. In general, a judicially imposed standard such as a numerical quota will be constitutionally acceptable if its referent or basis is a constitutionally cognizable standard. It is the existence of a referent standard that insulates judges from the charge of deciding cases on the basis of "an initial policy determination of a kind clearly for nonjudicial discretion."[1]

In a wide variety of cases, the use of standards requires a judgment about whether this or that particular standard most accurately reflects the underlying, accepted constitutional standard. (Do the "actual malice" and "public figure" standards in libel cases accurately reflect the standard of the First Amendment? Does the "clear and present danger" test? The current obscenity standards? The "public forum" standard? Does the Exclusionary Rule accurately reflect the standards of the Fourth and Fifth Amendments? Does sexual privacy reflect those and other guarantees? Etc., etc.) In most of these cases a judgment is required about the reasonableness of the nexus between the particular and the general standard, and/or between either of the standards and the particular application of it. (Does the death penalty violate the prohibition of cruel and unusual punishments? Does prosecutorial comment on the failure to take the stand violate the right against self-incrimination? Does the prohibition of abortions invade a woman's right to privacy? Is an airport, or a mailbox, a public forum?) Many of these cases involve difficult political, economic, or social assessments by the courts. (What, if any, degree of executive privilege is implied by the separation of powers? Is there a state-as-market-participant exception to the general rules under the Commerce Clause? Is a ban on advertising by pharmacists or lawyers constitutional? Should privately owned shopping centers be declared the functional equivalents of the earlier "Main Street" public forum?) In all these cases, as long as the courts' assessments are themselves reasonable—that is, are supported by facts and by plausible reasoning—then there is nothing "political" about the courts' decisions in the sense meant when one talks about "political questions."

In affirmative action cases, if it is once accepted that ideal-state, proportional quotas provide a legitimate basis for calculating real-world quotas in principle, then the underlying constitutional standard will have been established. By definition, again using the *Baker v. Carr* language, there will be no "initial policy determination of a kind clearly for nonjudicial discretion," but rather a judicially proper determination of constitutional principle. Thus, even in those cases in which the calculation and implementation of proportionality are complicated, there will be no inherent obstacle to judicial resolution. At some point, if the situation is particularly complicated and great precision is deemed necessary, a computer program might have to be enlisted, but, of course, judicial reliance upon technical data is neither unusual nor inappropriate.

It is possible to argue, however, that even where the actual applicant pool (in either education or employment contexts) is local or in-state, the calculation of proportionality ought to be made on the basis of the national population. If it is true that there would be absolutely no racial patterns in a completely nonracist society—including no residential patterns from locality to locality or state to state—then the imposition of a single, nationwide proportion for all places and all situations would be justified if judges and (other) policymakers were to go that far. This is not to say that there are no good reasons for using local populations in calculating quotas, but those reasons are often less compelling than they seem, so that if a judge *were* to employ the national population as the standard, it would not be arbitrary and nonminorities disadvantaged by it would have no grounds for objecting to it purely on the basis of racial fairness.

Thus, for instance, in the case of the state medical school that draws its students wholly from within the state, there seem, initially, to be good reasons for sticking with the state population as the base on which entering quotas are to be calculated. If nonminorities constitute, say, 75 percent of the state's population, it seems reasonable to let them compete for 75 percent of the entering seats in a state medical school. And because the state subsidizes the education involved, it seems reasonable to allow it to allocate the available seats among its citizens as long as it does so according to the racial makeup of the state. Even if the state's minority population is lower than that of the nation as a whole, it would seem to violate the spirit of federalism to force the state to subsidize the education of nonresidents merely because they were minorities theoretically entitled to a given proportion of all educational opportunities in the nation. Arguably there is an equity component in federalism; if a state cannot be said to be responsible for the racism of the nation, then it cannot fairly be made part of the remedy for that racism.

On the other hand, the nation is a whole, and the Fourteenth Amendment, addressed to the states, is a guarantee of national equality of opportunity, a guarantee that equality shall reign in all the states and from state to state. And the truth about equity in federalism is that states *are* responsible here. If blacks are under-represented in a given state's population there must be some reason, and that reason can only be a form of residual racism. Why do blacks not migrate to rural areas in the North and West in the same proportion that whites do? Why do blacks disproportionately migrate to urban areas in the Northeast? Racially unequal job and social opportunities are *state* problems, or at least are part of the state's responsibilities.

Or, if that stretches the concept of state action too far, the controlling principle in these cases can be stated negatively: no state has a right to profit from the racially differential hospitality of its society. Because a state's society has not been attractive enough to minorities to attract them in proportion to nonminorities in the twelve decades since the Fourteenth Amendment was ratified, it may not now claim the right to subsidize its educational opportunities disproportionately for the nonminorities who have chosen to live there. And nonminorities who would be disadvantaged by the imposition of a higher, national quota would have no legitimate complaint. Why should they profit from the fact that minorities have not felt welcome in their state to the same degree that nonminorities have? No matter how much of their tax money has gone to support state educational opportunities, those opportunities ought not be made available except on a basis of racial fairness, and in a union such as ours that means a national basis.

In theory, then, the argument for a single, national proportion in all things seems to be the correct one. But, even more than the essential proportionality argument, it is likely to be widely perceived as raising theory above all common sense. To impose on competing individuals the terms of a fair society inevitably seems more unfair as the conceptualization of the fair society becomes more abstract and divorced from reality. It is one thing to be asked to proportion benefits among those who are literally one's neighbors, those with whom one most directly and most obviously competes (or should compete); it is another to be asked to proportion benefits among strangers two or three thousand miles away. At the same time, compared to multiple, local proportions, a single, *national* proportion is likely actually to disadvantage minorities because the benefits typically targeted by affirmative action are disproportionately found in urban areas—where minorities currently disproportionately reside. But, of course, neither of these arguments ought to be within the notice of a judge searching for the proper standard. If the essential logic supports proportionality in principle, it supports proportionality in nationwide residence.

Applicant versus Labor Pool

Regardless of whether courts were to choose essentially local populations or the national population as their basis for figuring proportionality, they would face further complications. One of the easier questions likely to arise concerns whether, in employment cases, a judge should use the labor pool or the applicant pool as the base population. Recently, a federal district court judge held a large firm in violation of the law because it failed to live up to the terms of an affirmative action hiring order even though it had hired minority workers in proportion to the court-designated relevant labor pool. The court ruled that the firm should have used the job applicant pool as the basis for proportional hiring. Since minority individuals had applied for these blue-collar jobs substantially out of proportion to their numbers in the general population, the firm had failed to hire "proportional" numbers of minority workers. Interestingly, the firm appeared to accept the judge's decision willingly rather than to appeal it.[2]

Was the judge right? It is not hard to guess the reasoning underlying the decision. It seems reasonably clear that disproportionately large numbers of minority individuals applied for these blue-collar jobs because minorities are disproportionately unemployed, unskilled, and underrepresented in white-collar jobs. To have held that minorities are not entitled to a disproportionate share of what is left as a partial compensation for an undoubted effect of racism would have been to perpetuate the effect of that racism, to have compounded it. Even with the judge's order, it is clear that minorities would not be receiving their fair share of society's job opportunities; is it not intolerable to deny them even this partial compensation?

Courts more typically would have asked what the percentage of black blue-collar workers in the standard metropolitan area was, and then calculated the proportion of jobs to go to blacks on that basis.[3] That approach is preferable for two reasons. First of all, the judge's reasoning here would more often than not disadvantage minorities, since in traditionally segregated jobs—often the more desirable ones—minorities apply in small numbers, if they apply at all. More important, the judge's order constitutes a disproportionate quota which violates the rights of white blue-collar workers.

As with all disproportionate quotas, the judge's order attempts to give to the minority what it might be entitled to, but does it by taking disproportionately from one part of the offending society. It unfairly imposes on working-class whites a disproportionate burden of righting the wrongs of the larger society. Whites competing for any class of jobs have no claim of right to occupy, with other whites, a disproportionate share of any given class of jobs, but by the same token they do have a claim to occupy their proportionate share. White blue-collar workers have a right to the share of available, appropriate jobs that reflects their numbers in the whole society, because in a nonracist society white job seekers would apply for, compete for, and attain jobs *of all kinds* in proportion to their ratios in the general population.

In a nonracist society the applicant pool for all jobs would always reflect the racial percentages of the labor pool; there would simply never *be* racially disproportionate applicant pools for any jobs. If there *are* disparities, then, it can only signify that racism is at work assigning particular jobs to particular races. In an imperfect world, reliance on applicant pools will frequently result in skewed perceptions of fairness. Only the labor pool can tell a judge what the odds of employment would have been for individual job seekers in a racially fair world.

The judge's order constitutes the sort of decision that Justice Scalia found unjust and offensive when he spoke of his father and the "many white ethnic groups that came to this country . . . relatively late in its history." As he said, "it is precisely *these* groups that do most of the restoring. It is they who, to a disproportionate degree, are the competitors with the urban blacks and Hispanics for jobs, housing, education."[4] In this case, the district court judge was wrong and Justice Scalia would be right if he voted to overturn the decision on appeal.

In general, then, cases involving hiring quotas appear to be relatively unproblematical for courts wishing to employ the proportionality principle—at least, once the court has chosen between a national and a local standard. If the black population in the chosen base is 11 percent but the percentage of black plumbers is 20 percent, the relevant figure for determining quotas is the former. And by the same token, if blacks constitute 11 percent of the population but only 2 percent of systems programmers, the proper target quota ought to be 11 percent, not 2 percent.

It may well be that abiding by these quotas will result in too great a sacrifice of productivity simply because there are not enough qualified minority applicants to fill the quota. In that case, it will be a policy judgment whether to pursue the quota in the short or the long term. But if the employer, or university, does in fact choose not to fill positions with unqualified minorities, nonminorities may still not claim that they are in any principled sense entitled to the positions. They will still receive those positions as a result of the society's failure to encourage all of its citizens to prepare themselves for all of its roles. They will still be beneficiaries of racism. And by the same token, if the employer or university chooses to risk a degree of inefficiency in order to accomplish a proportional quota, nonminority members have no claim to the positions in question because of their greater merit. Their relatively greater merit is only partly due to their individual efforts; it is ultimately due to society's racist efforts on their behalf.

The Complications of Seniority and Repeat Applications in Hiring and Promotions

While straightforward hiring cases, and their analogue admissions cases, seem to present no general, insurmountable problems in calculating and implementing proportional quotas, the situation is not quite as simple as it seems. Further analysis suggests that in those cases even apparently disproportional quotas may sometimes not be unfair to current white applicants for jobs or promotions. Perhaps the best way to show this is to focus on cases involving either promotion quotas or their inverse, layoff quotas. With their narrower base populations, these cases show more clearly the range of possibilities courts would have to consider in calculating ideal-world fairness.

The Court has handed down two promotion-quota cases, United Steelworkers v. Weber and United States v. Paradise,[5] which illustrate better than any others the difficulties courts may face in applying the proportionality principle. In Weber, blacks had previously been discriminated against in hiring at a Kaiser aluminum plant, but non-discriminatory hiring in recent years had brought them into the least senior ranks. In 1974 a new craft-training program was announced that would train lesser-skilled workers for more skilled and better-paying jobs. Following standard practice, admission into the program was to be based on seniority—which would have meant that no black workers would have been eligible for the training program for several years. To avoid this perpetuation of racial disparity in the work force, the company and the United Steelworkers entered into an agreement that reserved for black workers half the places in the training program until such time as the percentage of blacks among the skilled workers at the plant approximated that of blacks in the local labor force—at that time 39 percent.[6] By a 5–2 vote, the Court upheld the agreement.

In the more recent *Paradise* case, the Court upheld another one-for-one promotion quota, this time ordered by a district court for the Alabama Department of Public Safety. The facts of this case are more unusual. As early as 1972 the district court had found that the department "engaged in a blatant and continuous pattern and practice of discrimination in hiring" state troopers. That finding was based in part on the "unexplained and unexplainable" fact that "in the thirty-seven-year history of the [state highway] patrol there has never been a black trooper and the only Negroes ever employed by the department have been nonmerit system laborers."[7] The court ordered the department to hire one black trooper for each white trooper hired until blacks comprised approximately 25 percent of the state trooper force, roughly the percentage of blacks in Alabama.

The department remained highly resistant, however, artificially restricting the size of the trooper force and the number of new troopers hired, and refusing to promote blacks beyond entry-level positions. In 1979 the district court, noting that "as of November 1, 1978, out of 232 state troopers at the rank of corporal or above, *there is still not one black*,"[8] ordered the department to include all ranks in measuring its compliance with nondiscrimination orders. As part of a consent decree at that time, the department promised to submit for the court's and plaintiffs' approval a promotion procedure for the position of corporal. Only after that had been validated would the department submit, in turn, promotion procedures for the positions of lieutenant, captain, and major. The promotion procedure for corporals was due within a year of the consent decree. It was agreed that whatever it was, it would not result in a selection rate for black applicants that was less than 80 percent of the selection rate for white applicants—e.g., if 10 percent of white applicants were selected, then at least 8 percent of black applicants would have to be selected.[9]

More than two years later—more than a year late—the department proposed a promotion procedure that relied heavily on written examinations. The United States and Paradise, a plaintiff in various challenges to the department since 1972, objected but agreed to allow the department to administer the test as part of some overall procedure yet to be approved. In October 1981 the department administered the written corporal's examination to 262 applicants, of whom 60, or 23 percent, were black.[10] The department then proposed to draw sixteen to twenty corporal promotions from the register of test results, in rank order. Since the highest-ranked black was number 80, no blacks at all would be promoted.

Obviously the proposed procedure did not meet the terms of the consent decree. The United States objected but did nothing beyond "suggest[ing] that the Department should submit an alternative proposal for making promotions in conformity with the 1979 and 1981 consent decrees."[11] The department refused, and no promotions were made in the next nine months. Finally, in April 1983, Paradise moved the district court for an order enforcing the terms of the two consent decrees.[12] Paradise asked for a one-for-one promotion order "until such time as the defendants implement a valid promotional procedure."[13] Before the district court ruled, the department submitted an *ad hoc* plan for promoting fifteen immediately needed corporals—eleven whites (or 73 percent) and four blacks (or 27 percent). Since the "percentage of blacks to whites reflect[ed] the percentage of blacks to whites who took the Corporal's examination," the department was finally meeting the terms of the consent decrees in the short term, but it still had not proposed a long-term, official procedure that would comply with them.[14]

It was in those circumstances that the district court agreed to impose Paradise's one-for-one quota. The court emphasized that the order would be in effect only until blacks were proportionally

represented (that is, at the rate of approximately 25 percent) in all
ranks "or the [department has] developed and implemented a promotion plan . . . which meets the prior orders and decrees of the
court."[15] The disproportionate quota was thus at least partially
justified as, and in effect was, a means of coercing the recalcitrant
department into agreeing to a permanent *proportional* quota. As such,
it seemed to have worked. The one-for-one quota had to be imposed only once. In subsequent promotions it was temporarily
suspended, allowing the department to promote both corporals
and sergeants on a roughly proportional basis. It remained, however, as a kind of Damocles' sword over the department's head
should it again violate the terms of the consent decrees governing
promotions, and the Reagan administration decided to intervene in
opposition to it on appeal. In strong and succinct language the
administration argued that

> this quota requires discrimination against innocent white state
> employees for no independently justifiable remedial purpose.
> The district court appears to have intended the one-for-one
> quota in part as an *in terrorem* device to compel the Department
> to adopt proper promotion procedures. In our view this puts
> the wrong gun to the wrong head, holding innocent white
> state troopers hostage for the purpose of ending the Depart-
> ment's alleged recalcitrance.[16]

The administration went further in rejecting even the district
court's goal of racial proportionality in all ranks in the department.
"This we believe goes well beyond a proper remedial purpose and
cannot be justified under the Court's decisions in *Sheet Metal Workers,
Wygant,* and *Regents of the University of California v. Bakke.*"[17] Thus, while
the administration's primary attack was on disproportionate quotas, and even though in passing it had accepted "that promotions
should . . . display approximate parity with the applicant pool," it
appeared to oppose, again, even proportional quotas in most cases.
The administration also relied on Justice Powell's "diffuseness-of-
the-burden" argument from *Wygant* and *Sheet Metal Workers,* namely,
that quotas are impermissible if they impose "unnecessarily heavy
burdens on a small number of identified white" individuals. Because "regular promotion and an orderly progression through the
ranks are an important aspect of a new entrant's career expecta-

tions," and because the one-for-one quota would "drastically diminish" and "blight those expectations" for "a defined group of individual white entrants," the Reagan administration argued that the ruling should be declared unconstitutional on those grounds also.[18]

Our analysis suggests, at least initially, that the Court's decisions in both *Weber* and *Paradise* were wrong, though perhaps not by much in the former and perhaps understandably in the latter, given the extreme circumstances. Had the agreement in *Weber* reserved 39 percent of the openings for black workers instead of 50 percent, the company's white workers would have had no ground for complaint. Since blacks made up 39 percent of the relevant labor force, that many black workers would have qualified for admission into the program under the rules of seniority had the initial hiring been fair. Under fair conditions every hiring cohort and every subsequent seniority cohort would be 61 percent white and 39 percent black, so that white workers would naturally have to compete with, and share promotions with, that proportion of black workers.

If black workers are absent from a given white worker's seniority cohort, that can only mean that that white worker's seniority has been artificially inflated due to racism. Had the white workers in that seniority cohort not been beneficiaries of racist hiring, enough blacks would have been hired before them and with them to comprise 39 percent of the equally senior and more-senior work force at the plant. The hiring line for those white workers would have been that much longer had eligible blacks not been kicked out of it, in effect moving whites ahead unfairly. Under such circumstances, those white workers should not receive all the promotions on the basis of that ill-gotten and exaggerated seniority.

But the quota upheld in both *Weber* and *Paradise* exceeded the proportion of blacks in the relevant labor force, and hence in the idealized seniority cohort. In upholding a one-for-one promotion quota in both cases, the Court has now twice approved a sort of remedial device, a "catch-up" quota designed to correct the racial imbalance in upper-level job categories faster than a proportional promotional quota would. Such quotas are not uncommon—they are likely to become more common because of the Court's decisions—and in terms of fairness to minorities, at least, they seem justifiable. But, like all disproportionate quotas, they may be unfair to white individuals because they compensate minorities for damage done by one party with the rights of an innocent third party. Disproportionate promotion quotas seek to remedy past abuses retroactively, but in so doing they risk "[putting] the wrong gun to the wrong head," as the Reagan administration said.

The real culprit here is seniority. Whatever else it accomplishes, in the context of affirmative action seniority acts to protect workers who have profited from prior racism. As long as seniority is held to be inviolate, courts will often be prevented from giving both minorities and junior white workers what they deserve. Whether the situation involves initial hiring or promotions (or layoffs), if the ill-gotten seniority of earlier-hired white workers is protected, then younger minorities and younger white job seekers and workers cannot both be treated fairly. For if minorities are to be given what they deserve immediately—proportional representation throughout the work force—yet seniority is not to be violated, the only option available to courts is a disproportionate quota that violates the rights of younger white workers and job seekers. Conversely, if the rights of the latter are to be respected along with seniority rights, then the minority cannot be given what it deserves until the senior workers leave their jobs, die, or retire.

In *Paradise*, for instance, we know that roughly 25 percent of the upper ranks of state troopers should be black, but before litigation those ranks were 100 percent white. This means that 25 percent of the all-white group of senior troopers were initially hired (and/or subsequently promoted) illegitimately. In terms of racial fairness, the ideal affirmative action remedy would be one that caused those 25 percent of senior troopers to be fired or demoted and replaced with black troopers. But even if the Supreme Court were to approve of such violations of the principle of seniority—which is unlikely—it is doubtful that a lower court could distinguish the 25 percent of senior whites who should not have been hired or promoted from the 75 percent who would have been hired and promoted even under racially fair conditions. Thus, to order a portion of the senior white troopers fired or demoted would at least flirt with arbitrariness. There is no way that such an order could avoid punishing theoretically innocent white troopers—or, more precisely, there is no way of knowing that innocent white troopers were *not* being unfairly punished.

This may slightly, but only slightly, overstate the case. Suppose a company hired or promoted workers on a regular, periodic basis—say, once or twice a year. Suppose further that the sole criterion was the applicant's score on an objective test of merit. Under those circumstances, a judge could retroactively determine which white applicants should have been hired/promoted and which should not have been. That is, simply by determining the percentage of whites who should have been hired/promoted in each period, and then referring to the test rankings of the applicants, a judge could reasonably conclude that in a nonracist world the top N white applicants would have been hired/promoted even if they had had to compete with an equally prepared and encouraged group of black applicants, but that the remaining whites hired/promoted would have been outscored by blacks.

The situation would be analogous, if not identical, to the admissions process in the *Bakke* case. It might also be similar to the situation in the *Paradise* case. Because in *Paradise* promotion to at least some (if not all) trooper ranks was ostensibly based on such objective test scores, that case is actually not a good one for illustrating the general rule. In *Paradise* the district judge might actually have been able to order the layoff or demotion of the relatively underachieving whites in all the trooper ranks. Such an order would be fair to white troopers only if the sole measure of merit had been the objective test and if that measure of merit was still available for distinguishing between those legitimately hired/promoted and those illegitimately hired/promoted.

Surely in the real world such situations are likely to be rare. Especially in relatively unskilled jobs, hiring is more often likely to be a matter of fulfilling minimum qualifications and being in the right place at the right time; and, outside of civil service, promotions are often based on more subjective measures of merit. Even where the initial hiring was based on a narrow, objective criterion, subsequent job performance will often have muddied the question of which white workers most deserve to be retained or promoted. Strictly speaking, such muddying is irrelevant to the question of racially fair layoffs. But racial fairness is not the sole good in a society—the apparent thrust of this volume notwithstanding—and many reasonable people will conclude that such situations are too morally messy to impose that single criterion of desert.

Given those reasons to respect even ill-gotten seniority, courts are faced with imperfect options. The second most immediate way of achieving representativeness in the upper ranks would be by using a 100 percent quota for future promotions. In *Paradise*, that would have meant promoting blacks in numbers equivalent to the 25 percent of "missing" black troopers. But that would mean that the 25 percent of the white troopers illegitimately hired would still be retained and accorded full seniority rights; if, in addition, another "25 percent group" were to be given the constructive seniority they deserved, then a junior white trooper hired under fair conditions would have up to 25 percent more troopers placed ahead of him or her than should be. That means that less-senior whites would be paying for the sins of the "excess" more-senior whites who cannot be identified and either demoted or fired.

One must say "up to" 25 percent because the calculation is muddied by the impossibility of knowing how many of the 25 percent of "illegitimately hired" senior whites would have been hired in subsequent hiring cohorts. To assume the extreme, if all of them had reapplied until they were eventually hired (or if they all had been put on, and had stayed on, a list of those to be hired as soon as openings occurred), then the white hiring cohort would have been expanded by that much—exactly to its point under racially unfair conditions. Under such conditions the junior white trooper in question would have gotten to the front of the white hiring line 25 percent later—that is, he or she would have exactly the same seniority relative to whites that he or she has now. If, but only if, these assumptions are true, then in a fair world the junior white worker would have less seniority than both the black "group of 25 percent" given constructive seniority and the white "group of 25 percent"— who would have less seniority than they have now *but still more than the junior white worker in question.*

If, but only if, the assumption of "successful repeat applicants" is true, then the imposition of a disproportional promotion quota could produce an actual seniority for the junior white worker that he or she would have had in an ideal world. Under those circumstances, a disproportional quota could conceivably provide him or her with exactly the chance of promotion he or she is entitled to. Strictly speaking, the quota would not actually be disproportional in that case, because the base population would have been expanded to include previous cohorts, as it should be whenever there

is "spillover" from one applicant cohort to another—as, by definition, there is any time there is a degree of successful reapplication.

Of course, it is not realistic to expect that as a general rule in such
cases every one of the theoretically displaced senior whites would
reapply until they were hired. Surely in most cases some of them
would have sought, found, and accepted other employment. That
means that in an ideal world junior white workers would not have
to compete with all of them in addition to the proportional percentage of the labor force that is black. Under fair conditions,
realistically conceived, the junior white troopers in *Paradise* would
not be less senior than 25 percent of black workers plus all those
white troopers.

If one assumes that under fair conditions *none* of the theoretically
displaced white troopers reapplied (unlikely but not inconceivable), then none of them would have seniority over the junior
white trooper in question. Under those conditions, the imposition
of a proportional quota (based on the current labor pool only)
would result in exactly the right number of people being given
seniority ahead of that trooper, while the promotion of even one
minority person beyond the proportional quota would be one too
many people given seniority.

Some degree of this uncertainty also infects cases involving initial
hiring. Suppose, to stay with the approximate facts of the *Paradise*
case, a company had refused to hire blacks in the past even though
blacks made up 25 percent of the labor force. Our earlier analysis
suggested that if a judge were to impose or approve a hiring quota
for all future hiring, the quota ought to be 25 percent: simple
proportionality in a simple case. But now suppose, *arguendo*, that the
company has historically hired workers regularly and has typically
hired 50 percent of the applicants immediately and placed the
other 50 percent on a "future-hire" priority list. Suppose further
that all those placed on the list chose to remain on it rather than
commit themselves to other permanent jobs, and that they were, in
fact, subsequently hired before new applicants. In that admittedly
unusual case, racially fair hiring practices would have produced up
to 25 percent more applicants as nondiscouraged blacks joined
earlier cohorts of white job seekers. More important, since all
applicants are ultimately hired, fair hiring practices would have
produced up to 25 percent more workers with seniority.

Again, one must say "up to 25 percent" because some of the job seekers might finally become discouraged as the ratio of initial hiring goes down and the length of the waiting list goes up. If the number of jobs stays the same, the waiting list would increase twice as fast as the applicant pool; thus if the applicant pool increased 25 percent, the initial hiring ratio would decrease 20 percent (from 50 percent to 40 percent of applicants) but the waiting list would increase 50 percent (from 50 percent of the original pool to 60 percent of a 125 percent pool—a number equal to 75 percent of the original pool). But it is not inconceivable that no one would become discouraged. That means that under racially fair conditions up to 25 percent more people might have been hired before any given white applicant in a current cohort. And that in turn means that it would not be unfair to a current white applicant if only black workers were hired until they were equivalent to 25 percent of the existing work force. It would not be unfair, that is, even if a temporary 100 percent quota were imposed, for the effect would be to give that applicant precisely the relative hiring seniority he or she would have had in a racially fair world.

These illustrations support the following set of principles: The calculation of a fair quota for either hiring or promoting will depend on the likely rate at which "illegitimately hired" whites with seniority would have been hired under conditions of fairness. The number of these theoretically successful white reapplicants may vary between zero and 100 percent. As the number approaches zero, the proper quota for new hiring or promotions approaches proportionality; as the number approaches 100 percent, the proper interim quota also approaches 100 percent.

The upshot of all this is that there will necessarily be a degree of uncertainty in calculating the proper quota in both hiring and promotion cases. Assuming that courts will rarely, if ever, be able to ascertain with any certainty just what conditions would have prevailed in an ideal world—i.e., what percentage of the theoretically displaced white workers would have successfully reapplied—they cannot calculate with any certainty just what percentage of black workers can fairly be hired ahead of new white workers, or given constructive seniority and promoted. All that the judges can know is that the number will lie somewhere between zero and the percentage of minorities in the labor force.

In many cases it will be too simplistic to assume that what is theoretically neat will have actually occurred, namely, that none of the illegitimately hired senior whites would have been hired. But only if none of the illegitimately hired whites would still be there under fair conditions is a simple proportional quota for hiring or promotions theoretically fair and correct. If *all* of them would still be there, then the theoretically correct quota is 100 percent until the work force (or the upper ranks) becomes proportional. And if *some* of them would still be there, then the fairest quota will be somewhere between proportionality and 100 percent. Perhaps *Weber* and *Paradise* were correctly decided after all.

In truth, the degree of uncertainty here can easily be overestimated. As a general rule, courts will find considerable guidance in the characteristics of the particular labor pool—the one from which the jobs in question are drawn. More specifically, the characteristics of actual, successful original applicants will suggest the likely degree of "successful reapplication" in the theoretically constructed ideal state. The more the successful applicants tend to be of a single age or at a single point in their careers, or have abilities that place them significantly apart from their peers, the less likely it will be that successful reapplication would occur under more competitive, racially fair conditions. That is, the more the successful applicants exhibit the characteristics of either a time-bound cohort—one that people move into and out of simply by aging—or a special-ability cohort—"the best and the brightest"—the less likely it is that repeated applications by an initially rejected applicant will succeed.

That is why, in general, undergraduate and graduate admissions, and professional hiring and promotion, are all relatively unproblematical compared with blue-collar hiring situations where minimum qualifications vie with persistence and luck in determining success. In most of the former cases, judges may confidently infer that to be once rejected by a particular institution is to be permanently rejected. In those cases, each admissions cohort, or each hiring or promotion cohort, ought to be essentially proportional, for in a fair world the disproportionate number of whites ahead of the cohort in seniority would have been reduced as a proportionate number of blacks were hired. Because qualified blacks would have literally replaced the relatively underqualified whites rather than supplemented them, the relative seniority of new-cohort members would not have been changed by a policy of racial fairness, and their admission, hiring, and promotion ought to simply reflect ongoing proportionality.

Moreover, even in problematical cases courts would still be able to impose a quota that *cannot possibly* violate the rights of innocent white workers. Courts would still be safe from the charge of unfairness to whites in imposing proportional quotas. Proportional quotas based on the racial proportions within the current labor force can never be unfair to white job applicants or junior white workers because if they err, they err on the side of presumptions in their favor. That is, proportional quotas in hiring and promotion will always reflect the assumption that none of the illegitimately hired senior white workers would have even reapplied under fair conditions, let alone successfully reapplied.

Only under that assumption would there be exactly the same number of senior workers ahead of a given junior white worker or job applicant in a fair world as there are now—the only difference being that in a fair world a proportional percentage of them would be black—and only under that assumption would there be exactly the same number of whites in the most recent applicant cohort. Under those presumed circumstances the junior white worker's odds of being hired or promoted would be the best they can be in a fair world: they would be determined by the ratio of whites to blacks in his or her actual labor cohort rather than by the need to first place "supplemental" blacks in the senior ranks along with all the whites currently there.

The imposition of a proportional quota based on assumptions most favorable to whites may, of course, be actually unwarranted. In that case, the quota will, strictly speaking, be unfair to black applicants or black junior workers. If some white applicants had successfully reapplied, then some of the black applicants would reapply, too, so logic argues that the current black applicant cohort would contain at least some individuals who had applied earlier. They are now, so to speak, "trying again," just as their white counterparts would have. Since any degree of successful reapplication means that the current applicant cohort is inflated with earlier, unsuccessful applicants, some of the blacks with whom first-time applicants are competing would have been hired earlier under fair conditions. That means that the imposition of a proportional quota now will subject blacks to diminished odds compared with those they would have faced had the earlier hiring not been racist.

Especially when hiring is mostly based on widely shared minimum qualifications, excluded blacks from earlier times can be expected to reapply now that discrimination has ended. A judge who imposes a proportional quota in order to avoid even the possibility of unfairness to whites may be assuming nonreapplication when that is not justified, and may in effect denigrate and subordinate the rights of blacks to those of whites. That is a serious charge that judges ought to keep in mind. If this analysis is correct, it may be impossible in at least some cases to know where overall fairness lies. But at least if the judge errs toward proportionality, there can be no complaint from those most commonly thought to be injured by affirmative action—namely, whites.

To the degree that courts can reasonably determine the likely rate of successful reapplication, they can confidently impose hiring and promotion quotas that will be fair to junior white workers and also approach fairness to minorities. The degree of fairness will then vary only with the degree of "unsuccessful reapplication," which represents the true number of senior white workers who are being retained illegitimately in places belonging to minorities.

Seniority, Repeat Applications, and Layoffs: The Stotts Case Revisited

With this calculus in hand, courts can also confidently deal with the most complex cases to come before them—those involving layoffs. Since layoffs are in a real sense the mirror image of hiring and promotion, and since seniority typically governs layoffs just as it does promotions and (by extension) hiring, the same principles can and should be used to determine when, if ever, seniority may be violated and, if it may, to what degree. The Court has handed down two major layoff cases, *Firefighters v. Stotts* and *Wygant v. Jackson Board of Education*.[19] Both held that seniority ordinarily may not be abridged in the name of affirmative action; any departure from strict seniority in layoffs is impermissible because it constitutes punishing "innocent" white workers with seniority. Our analysis suggests that stated that way—unconditionally, as a general principle—that holding is unwarranted. Because it is impossible from the record to tell whether *Wygant* involved a proportional or a disproportional layoff quota,[20] our discussion uses the former as illustrative.

In *Firefighters*, the city of Memphis had twice entered into consent decrees to increase the number of black employees in its fire department. Although the city did not formally admit past intentional discrimination in either decree, the disparity between blacks in the fire department and blacks in the local labor force had been striking. In 1974 blacks constituted approximately 32 percent of the labor force in Shelby County, Tennessee, but less than 4 percent of the fire department. The city acknowledged then that its employment practices "gave rise to an inference of race and sex discrimination,"[21] and committed itself to "a long-term goal of increasing minority representation" in each job classification in the department to levels approximating the level of minority representation in the local labor force.[22]

Between 1974 and 1980, the date of the second consent decree, the city's record was better, if still uneven. Blacks constituted 46 percent of all people hired or rehired—a disproportionate quota. However, because the number of new employees was relatively small, black employment in the fire department was still only 10 percent in 1980, while the black percentage of the labor pool had risen to 35 percent; and blacks had received less than 17 percent of all promotions.[23] Because Carl Stotts, a black captain in the fire department, felt that the city was still dragging its feet, he and others instituted the second suit. In the consent decree settling that suit, the city agreed to a (disproportionate) 50 percent interim hiring goal and a 20 percent interim promotion goal for qualified minorities.

Approximately a year after that accord was reached, however, the city announced that budget deficits would require personnel reductions in all its departments. In accord with the wishes of the firefighters' union, layoffs and demotions would follow the common "last-hired, first-fired" principle of seniority. Although the city's layoff proposal may not have been adopted with the intent to discriminate, it had a disproportionately adverse effect on blacks, since the vast majority of blacks had been hired only recently. Of sixteen lieutenants scheduled for demotion, for instance, fifteen were black, which would have resulted in the percentage of black lieutenants being reduced from 12.1 percent to 6.3 percent.[24] After

Stotts sought and received a temporary restraining order, the district court and court of appeals ordered the city to effect its layoffs and demotions without decreasing the percentage of blacks in the various ranks within the fire department. The city and the union appealed.

The case was argued mostly on technical and statutory rather than constitutional grounds (in particular, on the question of whether the district court's injunction violated the terms of the most recent consent decree), but the innocent persons argument was a critical element even there. In its *amicus* brief in support of the city and the firefighters' union, the Reagan administration argued that Title VII of the 1964 Civil Rights Act,[25] which prohibits discrimination in employment, nonetheless also prohibits federal courts from modifying "bona fide seniority systems" as part of a remedy for found discrimination. The administration argued that Congress intended to preserve seniority rights because "preservation of those rights serves two important concerns: protecting the stability of labor relations by maintaining the seniority system and *being fair to innocent incumbent employees*."[26] The latter reference was obviously to whites hired in earlier, discriminatory times who would be laid off even though they had more seniority than more recently hired blacks. The administration pointed out that the Supreme Court itself had "recently emphasized that, in crafting equitable relief under Title VII, courts must consider the legitimate interests of 'innocent third parties.' "[27] The administration argued, in fact, that no remedy was appropriate because there were no "specified victims" of discrimination—as opposed to blacks in general. But, again quoting the Court, "even in a case (unlike this one) in which specified victims of unlawful employment discrimination have been identified, a court, in determining their rightful place, is 'faced with the delicate task of adjusting the remedial interests of discriminatees and the legitimate expectations of other employees innocent of any wrongdoing.' "[28] Finally, and most emphatically, the administration argued:

> In the instant case, innocent firefighters were required to sacrifice not only their seniority, but also their jobs to persons who have never claimed to be victims of unlawful discrimination. As a result of the district court's decree, white firefighters with more years of service than black employees were furloughed

or demoted, thus creating a new class of victims, who were innocent of any wrongdoing, but were deprived of their rights under a valid seniority system.[29]

The administration's arguments apparently had the desired effects. The Court, speaking through Justice White, held that "Title VII protects bona fide seniority systems, and it is inappropriate to deny an innocent employee the benefits of his seniority in order to provide a remedy in [a] suit such as this."[30] The Court noted, as the Reagan administration had, that lower courts had also recognized the innocent persons argument and had "uniformly held that relief for actual victims does not extend to bumping employees previously occupying jobs."[31] Even the dissenters conceded that "the effect of the preliminary injunction was to shift the pain of the city's fiscal crisis onto innocent employees," and that the Court "has recognized before the difficulty of reconciling competing claims of innocent employees who themselves are neither the perpetrators of discrimination nor the victims of it."[32]

The question, then, is straightforward: Can white workers with more seniority than blacks be laid off in order to protect some racial balance in the work force from being upset? Frequently, as in *Stotts*, an affirmative action program will have been only recently put into effect, with the result that worker cohorts with the most seniority are disproportionately, if not completely, white. Often a racially fair quota will be present only among the least senior workers. If layoffs occur strictly according to seniority, the inevitable result will be to render the work force once again disproportionately white. Yet the Court held that *any* departure from strict seniority in layoffs was impermissible because it would constitute punishing "innocent" white workers with seniority. Because at least some of the whites in *Stotts* would not have had seniority had it not been for past discrimination, at least some of them were not entitled to have their jobs protected at the expense of black firefighters with less seniority. The problem for courts is to find those whites and to separate them, somehow, from whites who would have been hired even if blacks had not been discriminated against. More often than not, that simply cannot be done.

While even an order requiring that only whites be fired until the work force reflected the relevant labor pool might be constitutional under a compensatory justice or group entitlement analysis, such an order would have violated the rights of individuals in the class of least-senior whites. Because they would be asked to pay entirely for the sins of several "cohorts" of previous job applicants, their rights would be violated. This is true even though according to our logic it would appear that they would not have been hired in the first place if it had not been for racism. The truth is that some of them would have been hired in a nonracist society. Thus, *proportional layoffs* do not violate anyone's rights, whatever their seniority, because in a fair society the seniority of most white workers would be less, and would place them in jeopardy of layoffs along with a proportionate number of blacks. This is true of even the most senior white workers, but it is problematical to use disproportionate layoffs to achieve immediately a racially representative work force. Each "class" of workers should be treated as a cohort; otherwise, the sins of the elders are paid for by the younger workers, just as they would be if the University of California at Davis had attempted to make up for years of fault by accepting only blacks for a number of years.

The guiding principle for the Court in these cases should be that seniority, like everything else in a society, ought to obey the laws of racial proportionality, as it would in an ideal world. Each and every class of workers hired would, in that world, reflect the larger society's racial composition, so that any layoffs according to seniority would automatically result in the discharge of proportionate numbers of minorities and nonminorities.

If earlier generations of workers were hired discriminatorily, then in principle a given percentage of those workers can be said to have been hired when they should not have been. Those workers are not innocent; they have undue, excessive seniority, and that illegitimate seniority should not be used now to protect them from being laid off in place of blacks who should have been hired either in their places or ahead of them. Thus, if there were a way for courts to determine which of the earlier white workers would have been hired in a nonracist society and which would not, the courts would be fully justified in ordering the improperly hired whites laid off and in promoting blacks to their positions—in engaging in what the Reagan administration rightly called (and too strenuously opposed) "constructive seniority." The fairest layoff order (in terms of distributive justice) would be one that worked to *create* proportionality among all hiring cohorts, that is, one that laid off senior white workers until the racial proportion in their cohort matched that of the base population.

As in *Weber* and *Paradise*, then, it is clear that at least some of the whites in *Stotts* would not have had seniority had it not been for past discrimination. If blacks constituted 32 percent of the relevant labor pool as far back as 1974, then they should be represented at that rate in the upper ranks of the department rather than at their actual 4 percent rate. It follows that roughly 28 percent of the senior firefighters, all of them white, were not entitled to have their jobs protected at the expense of black firefighters with less seniority. As in those cases, the problem for courts is to find those whites and to separate them, somehow, from whites who would have been hired even if blacks had not been discriminated against. More often than not, that simply cannot be done.

The trouble is, as discussed above, that there is no calculus by which courts can separate those whites who should have been hired from those who should not have been hired, so that to order a portion of them laid off at least flirts with arbitrariness. Thus, while the fairest layoff order (in terms of distributive justice) would be one proportional among all hiring cohorts—i.e., it would lay off senior workers in the same racial proportion that it laid off junior workers—there is no way that such an order could avoid punishing theoretically innocent white workers.

The upshot of identifying exactly those who should have and should not have been hired is that courts must ordinarily be content with ensuring that layoffs be proportional overall. That means that recently implemented affirmative action hiring programs will be seriously undercut, if only temporarily. Moreover, the larger the disparity between the earlier hiring patterns and the affirmative action hiring quota, the greater the impact will be. Thus, for instance, if no minorities were hired during all the years when 90 percent of the work force was being hired and if 10 percent of the work force must now be laid off, then the work force will revert to 100 percent nonminority. Also, in cases where the affirmative action quota was itself disproportionate, as in *Stotts*, the impact is likely to be devastating—but then, the principle of proportionality, which is really the principle of individual fairness, would have argued against that quota in the first place.

When the most recently hired groups of workers are disproportionately white, it might seem that seniority rights could be
abridged with confidence. In that case, after all, it can be said that
some of those very workers were hired illegitimately, in place of
blacks. To strip them of seniority protection is not to strip them of
any right they are entitled to, since they shouldn't have been hired
in the first place. But here again, there is a problem separating the
innocent from the guilty. Suppose the least senior cohort is 90 percent white while the percentage of whites in the relevant labor
force is 80 percent. In that case, the cohort after layoffs should
also be 80 percent white. But how can one choose the extra white
workers to be laid off in order to achieve the resultant proportional worker cohort? Strict seniority—distinguishing by the min-
ute hired—will simply result in a microcosmic version of the unfairness outlined above: imposing the entire payback burden on
the least senior workers. In truth, whenever seniority is involved,
layoffs according to race will *always* result in potential unfairness to
individual whites for the simple reason that seniority overrides
original merit in hiring.

Thus a perfectly fair remedy will not normally be available—one
fair to both minorities and junior white workers—because some of
the seniority due minority workers is being held by undeserving
whites who cannot be isolated and removed from the seniority
ranks. But what is available in layoff cases is what is available in
many, if not most, hiring and promotion cases—namely, the ap-
proximation of fairness to both groups. As in hiring and promotion
cases, what really needs to be done to approach complete fairness
in layoff cases is to determine the likely rate of successful reapplication in the work force, for that in turn will determine the rate at
which minorities could be given preferential treatment in hiring
and promotion. And *that* rate is the inverse of the rate at which
minorities should be laid off.

To illustrate: Suppose that the district court in *Stotts* found that successful repeat applications among firefighters were highly unlikely.
To simplify things, let us suppose that the judge found virtually no
likelihood that unsuccessful applicants would subsequently reapply successfully, especially under the more competitive conditions
that racial fairness would produce. That means (virtually by definition) that at least 32 percent of the senior firefighters hired in earlier,

discriminatory times would not have been hired under conditions of racial fairness. Instead, they would have been outranked by qualified, undiscouraged black applicants who would have been hired instead.

Thus, even in a society that had always been racially fair, a given junior white firefighter would not be outranked by any more individuals than he or she is now. True, he or she would be outranked by blacks in numbers equivalent to 32 percent of the more senior firefighters, but he or she would also be outranked by that many fewer whites. With no net change in seniority under fair conditions, no black firefighter can fairly be given constructive seniority over that junior white firefighter without violating his or her rights. And by the same logic, any layoffs would also have to strictly follow actual seniority. And, as noted above, this means that recently implemented affirmative action hiring programs will be seriously undercut, if only temporarily, by layoffs in occupations where there is a low likelihood of successful repeat application.

There will, however, be many layoff situations in which courts would be justified in modifying seniority. To imagine the case at the other extreme, let us suppose that the district court judge in *Stotts* found a possible 100 percent likely successful repeat application rate. That means, again virtually by definition, that every one of the senior whites hired in earlier, discriminatory times would have eventually been hired even under conditions of racial fairness. Most of them would have less seniority than they now have, because qualified blacks would have been hired before them, but all of them would have more seniority than a given junior white firefighter. In addition, that junior white firefighter would be outranked by another group of at least 32 percent, all of them black, who would have been hired under fair conditions. All of this means that it would not be unfair to that junior white firefighter to immediately give constructive seniority to that 32 percent. Under fair conditions that junior white firefighter would not have been hired until all of the more senior whites, plus blacks equal to 32 percent more, had been hired.

If all that is true, then it is also true that it would not be unfair to that junior white firefighter to give layoff protection to blacks in numbers equivalent to 32 percent of the senior firefighters. It would not be unfair, that is, to lay off that junior white firefighter, along with a number of other white firefighters equal to 32 percent of the senior force, before laying off a single black firefighter. The reason is simply that in a fair world that number of blacks would have supplemented the ranks of senior whites. In a fair world, those white firefighters would have been in jeopardy of layoffs according to their actual seniority. Sher concluded that it is "largely irrelevant that many who are now entrenched in their jobs have already benefitted from the effects of past discrimination at least as much as the currently best qualified applicant will if reverse discrimination is not practiced."[33] But if our analysis is correct, that statement needs to be greatly qualified. Sher's reason for the alleged irrelevance of racial unfairness in the past is that the beneficiaries of it have usually not harmed the *current* minority applicants. If true, that fact would help to justify "singling out" the current applicants for some degree of "reverse discrimination," since the current non-minority applicants would then bear primary responsibility for the deficits of current minority applicants.

By ignoring the proportionality principle Sher missed the important point that in those cases the earlier unfairness is also irrelevant in determining *how much* discrimination against the current applicants is fair. If what has occurred in the past has not affected the current applicants (both black and white), then the determination of proportionality must proceed without reference to the earlier cohorts. This is another way of saying that when one cohort does not influence the chances of the other, the two should be kept separate for purposes of calculating proportionality.

But far more important, the earlier cohort *does* affect the later cohort by the extent to which its members would have successfully reapplied under fair conditions. Sher is "inclined to think there may be a case for reverse discrimination even" where the earlier unfairness has affected current applicants,[34] but that will *always* be the case, one way or the other. Since the degree of likely successful reapplication is actually a measure of the degree of the earlier unfairness—the lower the likelihood of successful reapplication, the greater the current number of illegitimate senior workers and, hence, the greater the degree of unfairness now—the determination of fairness in all current cases will be affected by the degree of earlier unfairness.

epilogue

The debate over affirmative action and quotas has continued apace since Ronald Fiscus completed his manuscript. Indeed, it can be said to have intensified, as is evident from the debates over proposed legislation in 1990 and 1991. Moreover, the debate will be with us for a long time to come. Since Fiscus developed this effort to sort out the arguments about elements of affirmative action, the rhetoric has, if anything, grown more fuzzy, not more precise, and the amount of heat generated by current controversy has not been matched by an increase in the light cast on the subject. This is not surprising, because political rhetoric seldom serves to increase enlightenment about a subject. Not only has the term *quotas* been misused (and overused), but compounding the rhetorical confusion is the substitution of *diversity* for *affirmative action*.[1] At the heart of the continuing confusion over terminology has been criticism of affirmative action, not only from white neoconservatives but also from some blacks, including Supreme Court nominee Judge Clarence Thomas during his tenure as chairman of the Equal Employment Opportunity Commission. Shelby Steele's magazine articles[2] and television appearances have made him one of the most recent visible individuals advocating such a position, in which he has joined Thomas Sowell, author of *Preferential Policies: An International Perspective*.[3]

This volume has, we hope, made a contribution toward clarity, although perhaps it is naïve to think that had its argument been heard, some of the distortion in rhetoric that did occur might have been prevented. Yet even were we able to increase the precision with which the term is used, the final word on affirmative action in general, and quotas in particular, cannot be stated. Nonetheless, some material on developments—political, judicial, and jurisprudential—in the time since the author completed this manuscript can be added; that is the purpose of this epilogue. Such developments have taken place at several levels. At one level, the Supreme Court has continued to develop its affirmative action jurisprudence, although perhaps in a way that has made it more difficult to mark the course of that jurisprudence. In *Metro Broadcasting v. Federal Communications Commission*, a case involving policies of the Federal Communications Commission (FCC) aimed at increasing the number of minority-owned radio and television stations, the Court upheld those policies—only one term after the *Croson* ruling had made it more difficult for cities to create set-aside programs for minority contractors. Although *Metro Broadcasting* was an important case, in the last few years the most important activity concerning affirmative action has taken place in the legislative arena, where efforts were made to overcome presidential opposition and rhetoric about quotas in order to overturn Supreme Court rulings on racial discrimination.

At another level, the innocent victims argument—that innocent whites are harmed by racial quotas—was further stated, perhaps more strongly (if not more persuasively) than before, when the Republican administration of President George Bush used it in opposition to legislation to correct a series of rulings by the Supreme Court during its 1988 Term that limited the chances for success of those seeking to use the statutes outlawing job discrimination. Indicative of the sway of the innocent victims argument is the headline of a 1991 newspaper opinion piece, "White Men Need Not Apply: Society's Newly Dispirited."[4] We will see the role of the "quotas" rhetoric when we examine the recent politics of affirmative action.

The third development has occurred in the jurisprudence of civil rights argumentation. Here we find creative efforts to develop arguments that justify action to protect civil rights. These arguments are, at least to some extent, based on a recognition that the innocent victims argument has enough political power to block further development of corrective civil rights action. Without canvassing the literature, we might point to one example: James Liebman's serious efforts to ground school desegregation on the notion that desegregation is necessary to undo widespread and long-standing deficiencies in our democratic political process, which have devalued the views of some of the nations' citizens—its racial minorities.[5]

Liebman advocates the "reformative theory" of desegregation, in which desegregation is seen as properly modifying the political system in which all people—white and black and brown—live. By "reform[ing] malfunctioning political systems," desegregation, seen in these terms, is not harmful to "assertedly 'innocent' white families," the "innocent victims" of affirmative action plans.[6] Liebman feels that "desegregation may—and to survive probably must—be seen as reconstructing a political process, in which we all share an interest, that has gone dangerously awry."[7] It has gone awry because, in placing obstacles to voting by minorities and in developing methods of diminishing the weight of their votes ("vote dilution"), whites have communicated the message "I am better than you," a message that must be replaced by "you and I are equally worthy" in the political sphere.[8] Arguments like Liebman's are necessary if efforts to vitalize desegregation and remove racial discrimination are to succeed. One wonders, however, whether they will be more successful in avoiding the distortion to which efforts to justify affirmative action have been subject.

Let us now turn to look in greater detail at the first two levels of developments noted above. We start with the Supreme Court's *Metro Broadcasting* ruling. Then we turn to recent politics—the debate surrounding the Civil Rights Act of 1990 and the short-lived change in policy with respect to scholarships for minority students.

The Metro Broadcasting *case.* The Supreme Court decided one major affirmative action case in its 1989 Term, and none in its 1990 Term (which ended in June 1991). The one case, *Metro Broadcasting v. Federal Communications Commission* (1990),[9] was to be Justice Brennan's last opinion for the Court before his retirement. The case involved a challenge to two aspects of the policies by which the FCC attempted to increase the number of radio and television stations owned by minorities. One was its "distress sale" program, in which prospective minority owners were able to buy radio and television stations when the commission had indicated it would revoke the owner's license or would, at the time of renewal, examine basic qualifications to hold the license. In the other policy the agency gave enhanced weight to minority ownership when competing applicants were being considered for a license in what are known as comparative proceedings.

By a vote of only 5–4, the Court sustained both policies. The majority found that both were substantially related to the government's interest in diversity in broadcasting and that neither placed impermissible burdens on nonminorities (the innocent victims issue). Thus neither program violated the equal protection component of the Fifth Amendment. Justice Brennan spoke for a majority including Justices Blackmun, Marshall, White, and Stevens (who also filed a short concurring opinion). There were two dissenting opinions—by Justice O'Connor for Chief Justice Rehnquist and Justices Scalia and Kennedy, and by Justice Kennedy, which Justice Scalia joined.

Given the Supreme Court's uneven course of decisions on affirmative action plans, and the generally limiting approach of the *Croson* majority only the previous term, the Court's action in *Metro Broadcasting* seemed somewhat surprising. The majority reached its conclusion by deciding that *Croson* did not undercut the Court's *Fullilove* ruling, which upheld a set-aside program in public works construction. As in *Fullilove*, the Court found it determinative that *Congress* had spoken: when Congress, having determined that an affirmative action program served important government interests, mandated such a program, the Court would give deference to Congress's findings. As Justice Brennan said in *Metro Broadcasting* about *Fullilove*,

> We held that benign race-conscious measures mandated by Congress—even if those measures are not "remedial" in the sense of being designed to compensate victims of past governmental or societal discrimination—are constitutionally permissible to the extent that they serve important governmental objectives within the power of Congress and are substantially related to achievement of those objectives.[10]

Justice Brennan conceded that the challenged policies were not intended to provide remedies for specific victims of discrimination. Instead the policies would increase broadcast diversity, which would redound to the benefit of all: "The benefits of such diversity are not limited to the members of minority groups who gain access to the broadcasting industry by virtue of the ownership policies; rather, the benefits redound to all members of the viewing and listening audience."[11]

The majority gave deference to both the FCC and Congress as to the policies' purpose. The FCC had not adopted the policies hastily but had considered alternatives, and its "conclusion that there is an empirical nexus between minority ownership and broadcasting diversity" was "a product of its expertise," deserving the Court's deference.[12] As if this were not sufficient, the availability of judicial review of the FCC's decisions—as in this case—was further protection against misuse of the policy. Congress, which endorsed the commission's policies "only after long study and painstaking consideration of all available alternatives," had "made clear its view that the minority ownership policies advance the goal of diverse programming."[13] Because the appropriations measures through which Congress required the FCC to retain the challenged policies were for short durations, Congress can easily reevaluate the policy and readjust it.[14]

The majority was convinced that the distress-sale policy would not create "undue" burdens for nonminorities; the burdens would be no greater than those involved in *Fullilove*. The agency's policy applied only "to a small fraction of broadcast licenses," and then only when the owner whose license was in question decided to sell rather than proceed to a hearing. Furthermore, if a competing application for that license was filed by a nonminority, the license could not be transferred via a distress sale, so nonminorities held the power to block application of the policy.[15]

One of the issues dividing the *Metro Broadcasting* majority and minority was the standard of scrutiny to be used in deciding the validity of the FCC's policies. Justice Brennan adopted a standard for "benign" racial classifications that, while higher than the lowest level of scrutiny—the "rational means" test—was lower than "strict scrutiny." Dissenting Justice O'Connor, however, accused Brennan of having adopted a standard little different from that for economic regulation. She argued instead for strict use of "strict scrutiny." Justice O'Connor held the "traditional requirement," from which the majority departed, to be "that racial classifications are permissible only if necessary and narrowly tailored to achieve a compelling interest."[16] Increasing diversity of programming was not such an interest, she said; certainly it was "too amorphous, too insubstantial, and too unrelated to any legitimate basis for employing racial classifications."[17]

Even when Congress had spoken, said Justice O'Connor, there was "no support in our cases or in the Constitution" for "application of a lessened equal protection standard to congressional action."[18] The congressionally mandated affirmative action plan approved in *Fullilove*, in her view, was an exercise of Congress's power to enforce the Fourteenth Amendment; *Fullilove* applied, at most, to "congressional measures that seek to remedy identified past discrimination." By contrast, the FCC plan and its congressional backing were "not . . . for any remedial purpose."[19]

Justice O'Connor did not focus on the innocent victims argument, but she did refer to it in attacking the majority's use of "benign racial classifications." Such classifications, "a contradiction in terms," were, "to the person denied an opportunity or right based on race, . . . hardly benign."[20]

Justice O'Connor found diversity of programming a value proper under the First Amendment but not under equal protection guarantees. Use of race in attempting to achieve that value led to impermissible equation of race with diversity of thought and came too close to outright racial discrimination to be constitutionally acceptable. Indeed, the notion that someone of a different race would produce different, and thus more diverse, viewpoints was unacceptable racial stereotyping.[21] Moreover, the FCC had available more precise ways of achieving diversity of programming; it could implement those on an individualized basis through its hearing process, instead of using race as a proxy for diversity.[22]

Justice Kennedy argued, in a shorter dissent, that the Court's majority had returned to the much earlier deferential review of legislative action found in *Plessy v. Ferguson* and was not insisting, as it had in the past, on a remedial rationale for policies like those challenged in this case. Like Justice O'Connor, Justice Kennedy argued that *all* racial classifications, no matter what their purpose, should be subject to strict scrutiny. Again like Justice O'Connor, he attacked the FCC's equation of racial difference with diversity of views. He went beyond these arguments, however, to voice several policy objections to affirmative action plans. One was that the "special preferences" in such plans "can foster the view that members of the favored groups are inherently less able to compete on their own." A second was that "opportunists" made such programs "targets for exploitation" by seeking the financial advantages the programs provide without increasing the benefits minorities actually receive from inclusion in the programs.[23] A further objection, and one about which he said the Court's majority had not been candid, was that racial preferences imposed a stigma on the classes of people affected by the program and created "animosity and discontent."[24]

Where does *Metro Broadcasting* leave us with respect to the state of the law on affirmative action? Just as this book is certainly not the last word on affirmative action, certainly *Metro Broadcasting* will not be the last pronouncement from the Court on the subject. That ruling leaves us only with the proposition that programs adopted by Congress will be given greater deference than those adopted by state and local governments, and the narrowness of the vote for the majority in that case, coupled with the departure of Justice Brennan, leaves even that ruling vulnerable to change. Far more numerous than affirmative action programs in which Congress has had a hand are those adopted elsewhere—by state and local governments and by a variety of other institutions, including colleges and universities, as well as by private employers.

Given the extent of controversy surrounding affirmative action, many more cases involving those entities are likely to be proffered to the justices for their consideration. As the cases in which *Croson* was applied to city and county set-aside programs work their way up the judicial hierarchy, there will be a need to clarify the standards for that type of affirmative action program. And, more generally, cases are likely to raise the question of the extent to which any institution wishing to develop an affirmative action program will need to demonstrate that past discrimination existed and that such discrimination is actually being remedied by the program.

The 1990 civil rights bill. The most recent use of "quotas" rhetoric came when attempts were made to reverse a set of decisions from the Supreme Court's 1988 Term. Those rulings—decried by the civil rights community as a disaster from the perspective of efforts to remedy job discrimination—were the following:

> *City of Richmond v. J. A. Croson Company* (1989),[25] in which the Court said that the city had failed to demonstrate a sufficient basis for its MBE (minority business enterprises) set-aside program for city construction projects.
>
> *Wards Cove Packing Company v. Atonio* (1989),[26] holding that a disparate impact violation of Title VII was not shown simply by a high percentage of nonwhite workers in one type of job within a company and a low percentage of them in another type, and holding that to win a disparate impact claim, plaintiffs must show a connection between a particular employment practice of the employer and the disparate impact.
>
> *Martin v. Wilks* (1989),[27] allowing white employees affected by a consent decree to intervene at a later date to challenge the decree.
>
> *Lorance v. AT&T Technologies* (1989),[28] determining that the time for bringing a claim that a seniority system, neutral on its face, is discriminatory begins when that system is adopted, not when individuals find they are negatively affected by it.
>
> *Patterson v. McLean Credit Union* (1989),[29] finding that while the Court's ruling in *Runyon v. McCrary* (1976)[30] (that 42 U.S.C. 1981 reaches discrimination in the formation of contracts) should not be overturned, Section 1981 does not apply to racial discrimination after hiring, that is, it does not apply to racial harassment during employment.
>
> *Price Waterhouse v. Hopkins*,[31] holding that once a plaintiff shows that an impermissible factor like race or sex played a part in an employment decision, the burden shifts to the employer to show it would reach the same decision if that factor were not considered.
>
> *Independent Federation of Flight Attendants v. Zipes* (1989),[32] holding that in civil rights cases, attorneys' fees may be awarded against losing intervenors in cases only when the intervention was legally frivolous.

Only two of these cases—Croson (discussed in this volume) and *Wilks*—directly involved affirmative action programs, and only one (*Croson*) changed the standards for adoption of an affirmative action plan, although *Wilks* is relevant to the innocent victims argument because, in employment discrimination cases concerning governmental units, it allows disaffected white males to challenge consent decrees at any time. Yet the full set of cases, because of their collective "weight," have produced a greater impact on the civil rights community than each would have if they had appeared at different times.

Unlike the reading some gave it at the time, including some involved in challenges to plans in other cities, *Croson* continued the Court's approval of remedies that reach beyond particular instances of discrimination. Such affirmative action plans, at least if developed by state and local governments, would have to be placed on a firmer foundation—would have to be "narrowly tailored," in Justice O'Connor's words—but were still permissible.[33]

In terms of the use of "quotas" rhetoric, the most important case was *not* an affirmative action case but *Wards Cove v. Atonio*. This case initially was less visible because of its technicality and because it involved the issue of "burden of proof" in job discrimination cases—an important, nay crucial, matter but one difficult for most nonlawyers to comprehend. *Wards Cove* seemed to undermine the Court's first major Title VII pronouncement, the 1971 ruling in *Griggs v. Duke Power Company*,[34] in which the Court had supported "disparate impact" attacks on employers' employment practices. It did so in two ways. One was the requirement that instead of showing that employment practices (taken collectively) had a racially disparate impact, plaintiffs had to show the *specific practice* that produced that impact. The other was a shift in the burden of proof: whereas in *Griggs*, once disparate impact was shown, the burden shifted to the employer to show that the employment practices were relevant to the particular job, in *Wards Cove* the Court ruled that although the employer had to produce evidence that there was legitimate business justification for the practices that had been challenged, the plaintiffs still had to carry the ultimate burden of persuasion concerning the claim of discrimination.

Almost immediately, members of Congress introduced legislation to overturn or alter the Court's actions in the key cases noted above. (Although *Hopkins* had been a partial victory for civil rights forces, they wanted the statute amended so that an employer would be liable for discrimination if race, sex, or other prohibited factors played a role in an employment determination even if other factors were also a part of the decision.) In addition, the proposed law would have allowed women, religious minorities, and the disabled to seek compensatory damages and punitive damages in suits complaining of intentional discrimination against them. As a result of compromises during the legislative process, punitive damages would have been limited to the larger of two figures: $150,000 or the total of compensatory damages and back pay.

The civil rights community and the administration were not at odds with respect to reversal of all the Court's rulings. In particular, there was agreement that the Court's reading of Section 1981 in the *Patterson* case was erroneous and that racial harassment of a worker should be actionable under that statute—that such harassment did affect the ability of a person to enter into a contract without regard to race; likewise, failure to promote someone on racial grounds was an impediment to forming a new contract and thus should be within the ambit of the statute, not—as the Court had said—a matter subject to the formation of the contract. The administration also agreed that *Lorance* should be overturned, so that the statute of limitations for challenges to seniority systems would not begin to run until the practical application of such systems was felt.

Wards Cove became the focus because of the administration's position that it would be impossible for employers to comply with the disparate impact standard embodied in the legislation without using racial (and gender) quotas in hiring. Indeed, President Bush vetoed the Civil Rights Act of 1990 for "introduc[ing] the destructive force of quotas into our national employment system," despite language resulting from the legislative process that the new law should not "be construed to require or encourage quotas"—language parallel to that in the 1982 reenactment of the Voting Rights Act that the law not be interpreted to require "proportional representation," the buzzword in the voting arena equivalent to "quotas" in employment or education.

The administration's claim was, in part, that businesses would have to adopt quotas to avoid extensive litigation over hiring practices. The question of avoiding litigation is not new—it did not appear suddenly with this proposed legislation. The reality underlying the apprenticeship program established by Kaiser Aluminum and the Steelworkers, upheld in the *Weber* case, was that without such a program the company was open to suit by black plaintiffs who, on winning, might have obtained more substantial remedies from a judge than the plan provided. The Supreme Court, in upholding this purportedly "voluntary" plan, was undoubtedly also not unaware of litigation that would result were the Court to have rejected such adjustments in the workplace.

Quotas may not have been the only reason for the president's veto; the president's proposal also set lower limits on damages than did the bill passed by Congress. There was also some skirmishing as to whether the proposed legislation simply restored the status quo ante *Griggs* or actually facilitated victories by plaintiffs in employment discrimination suits.[35] The relationship between a characteristic of a potential employee and job performance would have to be "significant," not just "manifest," to be used to disqualify the job seeker. Plaintiffs would not have to show which particular employment practice had a disparate impact if companies failed to document the effect of particular practices. This distinction, if not merely semantic, was nonetheless not as significant as the concern, real or imagined, about the quota-forcing effects of the legislation.

An attempt to override the president's 1990 veto failed. The debate did not abate, however. It continued into the next year when the bill was reintroduced. Initially the 1991 version appeared without some of the provisions added as compromises in 1990, but after it was again opposed by the administration for requiring quotas, the politics of the situation again led the bill's advocates to insert language barring quotas. This time there was an additional issue, with the rhetorical label "race norming." In this practice, more officially called "within-group score conversion," state employment agencies rank test results separately for African Americans, Hispanics, and all others (including whites); in short, the percentiles are figured separately for each of the three groups rather than for all those taking the test, because the latter would place many African Americans and Hispanics in very low percentiles. Although the practice was not new, it burst on the scene during consideration of the 1991 version of the proposed civil rights legislation, immediately prompting calls that it be abolished and leading, as with the "quotas" issue of which it is a cousin, to efforts by the bill's supporters to limit race norming.[36]

Scholarships for minorities. Another aspect of affirmative action, seemingly far from quotas and instead part of the effort to attract minorities to higher education in greater numbers, also became embroiled in political controversy: the practice of offering some scholarships to minority students alone. In late 1990, Assistant Secretary of Education for Civil Rights Michael L. Williams stated that under the Department of Education's interpretation, setting up scholarships for minority students would probably violate Title VI—the provision of the 1964 Civil Rights Act outlawing discrimination by those entities receiving federal funds. Supreme Court rulings on quotas apparently played a part in Williams's action; he cited the *Croson* affirmative action case and *Bakke*, using from the latter the idea that race could not be the exclusive basis for university admissions decisions.[37] Williams's interpretation certainly diverged from past government interpretation, under several administrations, which had allowed such scholarships as part of a financial aid program that was nondiscriminatory as a whole.

That Williams acted on his own, without presidential approval or knowledge, helps explain why this new policy did not last long. Immediate and strong criticism met the announcement of Williams's interpretation. The White House immediately tried to distance itself from the new policy, although at first, and for some time thereafter, there was no outright reversal; instead there was an initial backtrack to a distinction between scholarships from private funds (allowable) and those from general university funds (not allowable). This fallback position, coupled with lack of certainty as to when the new (or newest) policy would begin, did nothing to reduce criticism of the administration, with the U.S. Commission on Civil Rights among those asking for reversal of the new policy. The nomination of a new secretary of education, former Tennessee governor Lamar Alexander, provided cover for the retreat, as Alexander told the Senate committee considering his nomination that he would suspend and reevaluate the controversial policy as soon as he took office, and he did just that.

Alexander did, however, question some efforts at "diversity"—or affirmative action—in higher education, most particularly when he deferred continuing the recognition of the Middle States Association of Colleges and Schools, in part because that accrediting organization had, in its accreditation evaluations, been taking into account affirmative action hiring programs and curriculum diversity. Also of a piece with the minority scholarship issue was an informal opinion letter from the Equal Employment Opportunity Commission saying that recruitment programs for minorities (minority summer clerkships and job fairs) violate Title VII if exclusively for minorities, although apparently if the recruiting mechanisms were targeted on minorities rather than exclusively for them the efforts would be considered legally acceptable.[38]

This series of events does indicate the entanglement of such matters in politics—within the administration as well as between Democrats and Republicans.[39] Certainly the political appeal of limits on programs benefiting minorities was one stimulus to Williams's pronouncement. That it happened only a couple of months after President Bush's veto of the Civil Rights Act of 1990 is perhaps not accidental; certainly the discussion of quotas created an atmosphere in which a government official could feel sufficiently secure to announce such a policy change. The position announced by Williams retains considerable appeal among conservatives; evidence is the suit by the Washington Legal Foundation against Alexander and Williams for not proceeding against colleges with scholarships reserved for minorities.

In this vein, it is interesting to note that politics and ideology clashed in 1991 during the decennial legislative redistricting exercise that follows each census. The Republican National Committee, seeing a way to increase the number of Republican legislators, provided assistance to African American legislators and interest groups who wished to create districts with strong African American majorities that would be quite likely to elect African American legislators; this would require concentrating African Americans in a limited number of districts. Because African Americans tend to vote Democratic, such concentration would also facilitate electing Republicans from more of the remaining districts. Thus the interests of the African Americans (at least if those interests are defined in a certain way) and of the Republicans would be convergent.

Some time into this process, however, some Republican conservatives began to question whether this trade-off was ideologically acceptable. The reason: to engage in this activity meant accepting the notion that in some districts there should be a "supermajority" of a certain race in order to guarantee representation by someone of that race. This was acceptance of affirmative action in the voting context, something against which the conservatives had argued when the Voting Rights Act had been applied to "vote dilution" because they felt it led to "proportional representation"—with such objections leading to language in the 1982 renewal of the Voting Rights Act to bar just such "proportional representation."

As these paragraphs were written in August 1991, the final word had not been written on the affirmative action stories described here. The minority scholarship issue continued to simmer, although on a back burner. President Bush had rejected a compromise civil rights bill proposed by a moderate Republican senator. This left for late in the year, and probably the following year, if then, the passage of any legislation to reverse the thrust of the Supreme Court's restrictive employment discrimination rulings. Indeed, some said the president was concerned less with having any legislation than with positioning himself for the 1992 election.

The Supreme Court, although not issuing any rulings on affirmative action during the 1990 Term, nonetheless became a focus of debate about affirmative action. This was because at term's end Justice Thurgood Marshall, the Court's first African American, retired and President Bush nominated Judge Clarence Thomas of the U.S. Court of Appeals for the District of Columbia, another African American, to replace him. The president asserted that race had nothing to do with his choice, but it was immediately clear that the president, despite his objection to "quotas," did have a quota in mind—that there was one "black seat" on the Court. Particularly after Bush said he had not used race as the basis for his choice, it became like the child's game "Don't Think of Elephants." As Jack Greenberg, a former NAACP Legal Defense Fund director, said of that game during Supreme Court oral argument in a Mississippi school desegregation case in which school officials said they were not taking race into account, "All the children do is think of elephants."

The president obviously also had on his mind Judge Thomas's outspoken opposition to affirmative action programs during Thomas's tenure as chairman of the Equal Employment Opportunity Commission (EEOC). This further injected the issue into the confirmation process. Stories about Judge Thomas having benefited from affirmative action programs, for example, in his admission to Yale Law School, a benefit he at times admitted, were also central to postnomination discussion. Even if Judge Thomas had not had a clear record on such matters, or if he had not spoken out about them, his nomination would certainly have focused on affirmative action, quotas, and other questions of race policy. The nomination served to confound the civil rights community, with African American groups initially unsure of what action to take, but after examination of his record the NAACP and other civil rights advocates opposed the nomination.

The absence of a Supreme Court ruling on affirmative action after *Metro Broadcasting* is undoubtedly only a temporary silence. Affirmative action cases are available on the Court's docket for the justices to accept if—more likely, when—they wish to say more on the subject. And they are likely to say more. Whether or not *Metro Broadcasting* was the Supreme Court's last decision upholding an affirmative action plan, the Court majority's increasing conservatism makes it likely that any ruling by the justices on affirmative action will constrict, not expand, it.

The Court's word, while central to the affirmative action debate, is not the only one to be heard on the subject. The description in this epilogue of legislative activity should make that clear. Whatever the present state of the law, all who have a concern for the future of American society—public officials and private citizens alike—will have to deal with the affirmative action issue. As they try to grapple with it, all can well heed the words of Ron Fiscus.

notes

Editor's Preface

1 See, for example, Days, "Fullilove," 96 *Yale L.J.* 453 (1987).
2 Freeman, "Legitimizing Racial Discrimination through Anti-Discrimination Law," 62 *Minnesota L. Rev.* 1049 (1978).
3 Cain, "Voting Rights and Democratic Theory: Toward a Color-Blind Society?" (Paper delivered at the Conference on Twenty-fifth Anniversary of the Voting Rights Act of 1965, The Brookings Institution, Washington, D.C., 19 October 1990), 1.
4 *Id.*, 18.
5 Liebman, "Implementing Brown in the Nineties: Political Reconstruction, Liberal Recollection, and Litigatively Enforced Legislative Reform," 76 *Virginia L. Rev.* 349, 369 (1990).
6 *Id.*
7 Some of the basic argument of that project appears as "The Constitution at 200," 23 *Polity* (forthcoming, Winter 1991).
8 The first is Stover, *Making It and Breaking It: The Fate of Public Interest Commitment during Law School,* ed. Howard S. Erlanger (Urbana: University of Illinois Press, 1989).

Introduction

1 *DeFunis v. Odegaard,* 416 U.S. 312 (1974); and *Regents of the University of California v. Bakke,* 438 U.S. 265 (1978).
2 The cases are *Firefighters v. Stotts,* 467 U.S. 561 (1984); *Wygant v. Jackson Board of Education,* 476 U.S. 267 (1986); *Local 28, Sheet Metal Workers International Association v. Equal Employment Opportunity Commission* [hereinafter EEOC], 478 U.S. 421 (1986); *Local Number 93, International Association of Firefighters v. City of Cleveland,* 478 U.S. 501 (1986); *United States v. Paradise,* 480 U.S. 149 (1987); and *Johnson v. Santa Clara County,* 480 U.S. 616 (1987).

3 *Wygant* and *Paradise* were decided 5–4; Justice Powell wrote the plurality opinion in the former. In *Stotts* he supplied the fifth vote for the majority opinion of Justice White; Justice Stevens concurred on narrower grounds.

4 In one, *Martin v. Wilks*, 109 S.Ct. 2180 (1989), the Court held that court-approved affirmative action agreements—*e.g.*, consent decrees—may subsequently be challenged by white or male individuals who feel they have been harmed by the agreements. The ruling was widely viewed as making it more difficult to resolve affirmative action disputes in favor of minorities and women. But the decision involved statutory rather than constitutional interpretation; it offered no additional Court analysis of affirmative action *per se*. For that reason, it need not, and will not, be discussed further in this volume (but see Epilogue, p. 120).

The Court also denied review in two affirmative action cases. In one case the court of appeals had struck down an affirmative action plan involving a quota; in the other case another court of appeals had upheld a similar plan. See *City of South Bend v. Janowiak*, 836 F.2d 1034 (7th Cir. 1988), cert. denied, 109 S.Ct. 1310 (1989); *Higgins v. City of Vallejo*, 823 F.2d 351 (9th Cir. 1988), cert. denied, 109 S.Ct. 1310 (1989).

5 *City of Richmond v. J. A. Croson Co.*, 109 S.Ct. 706 (1989).

6 Probably the least arbitrary first round of the public debate would be the congressional debate surrounding the passage of the Civil Rights Act of 1964. See in particular 110 *Congressional Record* 6548 (remarks of Senator Humphrey); id., at 7204 (remarks of Senator Clark); id., at 7379–80 (remarks of Senator Kennedy). This legislative debate, as it applied to Title VI, was reviewed and itself debated by the Supreme Court in *Regents of the University of California v. Bakke*, 438 U.S. 265, 281–87 (1978) (opinion of Powell, J.); at 328–50 (opinion of Brennan, J.); and at 413–21 (opinion of Stevens, J.). Title VII was reviewed and debated in *United Steelworkers v. Weber*, 443 U.S. 193, 200–207 (1979) (opinion of the Court by Brennan, J.); at 219–55 (opinion of Rehnquist, J., dissenting); in *Firefighters v. Stotts*, 467 U.S. 561, 579–83 (1984); in *Sheet Metal Workers v. EEOC*, 478 U.S. 421, 445–79 (1984) (opinion of Brennan, J.); at 489–99 (opinion of O'Connor, J.); and in *Johnson v. Santa Clara County*, 480 U.S. 616, 657–77 (1987) (opinion of Scalia, J., dissenting).

7 To mention merely the law journal commentaries provoked by the Court's decisions would be a substantial and even tedious undertaking. As of mid-1987, the *Index to Legal Periodicals* listed over two hundred commentaries on affirmative action since *DeFunis*. The ILP does not, of course, catalogue scholarly journals in philosophy, economics, sociology, or political science, all of which carried numerous commentaries on affirmative action during that period. Nor does it include entire books on the subject, of which there have been several. Under the circumstances, it seems slightly preposterous to cite anything at all here. Nonetheless, one can at least cite those works within the field of constitutional law that seem to have been most influential. Thus, Gunther's widely used casebook lists the following "sampling of the extensive pre-Bakke commentary on the constitutionality of color conscious admissions programs": O'Neil, "Preferential Admissions: Equalizing the Access of Minority Groups to Higher Education," 80 *Yale L.J.* 699 (1971); Graglia, "Special Admissions of the 'Culturally Deprived' to Law School," 119 *University of Pennsylvania L. Rev.* 351 (1970); Bell, "In Defense of Minority Admissions Programs: A Response to Professor Graglia," 119 *University of Pennsylvania L. Rev.* 364 (1970);

Sandalow, "Racial Preferences in Higher Education...," 42 *University of Chicago L. Rev.* 653 (1975); Posner, "The *DeFunis* Case and the Constitutionality of Preferential Treatment of Racial Minorities," 1974 *Supreme Court Rev.* 1; Greenawalt, "Judicial Scrutiny of 'Benign' Racial Classifications in Law School Admissions," 75 *Columbia L. Rev.* 559 (1975); and the symposia on DeFunis in 60 *University of Virginia L. Rev.* 917 (1974), and in 75 *Columbia L. Rev.* 483 (1975). Gunther also cited Ely, "The Constitutionality of Reverse Racial Discrimination," 41 *University of Chicago L. Rev.* 723 (1974); and Kaplan, "Equal Justice in an Unequal World: Equality for the Negro—The Problem of Special Treatment," 61 *Northwestern University L. Rev.* 363 (1966). Gunther, *Constitutional Law*, 10th ed. (Mineola, N.Y.: Foundation Press, 1980), 803, nn. 1–3.

For a useful annotated bibliography of pre-1983 works in law and philosophy, along with an interesting text, see Greenawalt, *Discrimination and Reverse Discrimination* (New York: Alfred A. Knopf, 1983). One interdisciplinary symposium of note not listed there is 26 *Wayne L. Rev.* 1199 (1980). Among the most recent commentaries, see in particular Fallon and Weiler, "*Firefighters v. Stotts*: Conflicting Models of Racial Justice," 1984 *Supreme Court Rev.* 1; Sullivan, "Sins of Discrimination: Last Term's Affirmative Action Cases," 100 *Harvard L. Rev.* 78 (1986); and, for an atypical perspective, Days, "Fullilove," 96 *Yale L.J.* 453 (1987).

8 This argument in particular has found expression in the opinions of the Supreme Court. Various members of the Court have argued that affirmative action programs can and do stigmatize their beneficiaries. See *Fullilove v. Klutznick*, 448 U.S. 448, at 545, 547, 552–53 (1980) (Stevens, J., dissenting); *id.*, at 531 (Stewart, J., dissenting); *United Jewish Organizations v. Carey*, 430 U.S. 144, 173–74 (1977) (Brennan, J., concurring in part); *Regents of the University of California v. Bakke*, 438 U.S., at 298 (1978) (opinion of Powell, J.); *DeFunis v. Odegaard*, 416 U.S. 312, 343 (1974) (Douglas, J., dissenting); *City of Richmond v. J. A. Croson Co.*, 109 S.Ct. 706, 733–34 (1989) (Stevens, J., concurring in part). See also Professor (now Justice) Scalia's pointed remarks in "Commentary—The Disease as Cure," 1979 *Washington University L.Q.* 147, at 153; and those of Professor (later Judge) Posner, "The DeFunis Case," 17 and n. 35. These arguments were largely endorsed by the Reagan administration in its attack on affirmative action. See, for instance, Brief for the United States, *United States v. Paradise*, no. 85–999, at 37 and n. 18.

9 Goldman, *Justice and Reverse Discrimination* (Princeton, N.J.: Princeton University Press, 1979), 231; see also 90–91, 114–15. Also representative of explicit endorsements of the innocent persons argument are the conclusions of Fallon and Weiler, "Firefighters v. Stotts," 14, 23, 27. For similar arguments about the unfairness of affirmative action when applied to innocent persons see Gross, *Discrimination in Reverse: Is Turnabout Fair Play?* (New York: New York University Press, 1978); and Vetterling, "Some Common Sense Notes on Preferential Hiring," 5 *Philosophical Forum* (Boston) 320 (1973–74).

10 See Sullivan, "Sins of Discrimination." This trenchant analysis of the Court's decisions attributes the Court's problems with "the perception of innocence" to its reliance on "the paradigm of sin":

> The problem with sin as the predicate for affirmative action is...that it keeps alive protests about windfalls to nonvictims and injustice to innocents. The

> Court held those protests at bay [during the 1986–87 term], but not by expanding the concepts of white sin or black injury, as it might well have done. Rather it left behind a doctrine of sin doomed to partial success—a doctrine in search of perpetrators but not of victims, and open still to cries of white innocence. (95–96)

As even this elegant summation suggests, Sullivan's formulation of the problem sometimes makes it appear that white innocence is merely a chimera caused by the Court's bumbling. However real and substantial it may be, Sullivan argued that it can be overcome by a forward-looking justification of affirmative action. By contrast, the argument advanced here is that claims of innocence are sometimes valid and sometimes not, but when they are valid, no principle of equal protection can justify overriding them (see pp. 44–50 in this volume).

11 448 U.S. 448, 514–15 (1980) (Powell, J., concurring).

12 *Wygant v. Jackson Board of Education*, 476 U.S. 267, 280–81 (1986).

13 Id., at 282–83 (opinion of Powell, J.); emphasis in original.

14 *United States v. Paradise*, 480 U.S. 149, 188 (1987).

15 Id., at 188–89.

16 443 U.S. 193, 208 (1979).

17 See, for instance, his concurring opinion in *Wygant*: "Whatever the legitimacy of hiring goals or quotas may be, the discharge of white teachers to make room for blacks . . . is quite another matter" (476 U.S., at 295 [White, J., concurring in the judgment]).

18 See *Wygant*, 476 U.S., at 294 (O'Connor, J., concurring in part and concurring in the judgment).

19 Sullivan, "Sins of Discrimination," 95.

20 Id.

21 Id.

22 480 U.S. 616, 662, 674 (Scalia, J., dissenting).

23 Greenawalt, *Discrimination and Reverse Discrimination*, 53.

24 This definition is sufficient only for equal protection purposes, since there are likely to be other requirements of distributive justice given other considerations. Thus, for instance, there is a well-known debate whether in a Rawlsian system a highly talented or exceptionally intelligent or industrious individual could claim certain benefits or advantages even if the conditions under which they were obtained were fair. Some, including Rawls himself, have emphasized that the Rawlsian system requires that even fairly obtained advantages be forgone if, crudely speaking, they do not advantage everyone to some extent. Given the "veil of ignorance" in the "original position," the argument goes, no one would rationally choose to permit such advantages. Others have argued that the Rawlsian system would permit substantial inequalities in real life, and have criticized it for that reason. Whichever side is correct, it seems clear that some conceptions of distributive justice—but not others—would prohibit the attainment of "excessive" benefits or advantages even if they were obtained under conditions of fair competition.

25 For essentially compensatory justice defenses of affirmative action, see Thomp-

son, "Preferential Hiring," 2 *Philosophy and Public Affairs* 364 (Summer 1973); Bayles, "Reparations to Wronged Groups," 33 *Analysis* 17 (1973); Taylor, "Reverse Discrimination and Compensatory Justice," 33 *Analysis* 185 (1973). See also *Bakke*, 438 U.S., at 387–402 (opinion of Marshall, J., concurring in part and dissenting in part).

26 Greenawalt, *Discrimination and Reverse Discrimination*, 53–54. See also Gross, *Discrimination in Reverse*, which argues that compensatory programs are morally unjustifiable if extended generally to minorities; that is, only individual victims of harm may justifiably be compensated.

27 Kaplan, "Equal Justice in an Unequal World," 363, 373.

28 *Id.*, at 374.

29 Fallon and Weiler, "*Firefighters v. Stotts*," 27. See also Sher, "Justifying Reverse Discrimination in Employment," 4 *Philosophy and Public Affairs* 159, 160–62 (1975); Sullivan, "Sins of Discrimination," 92.

30 Scalia, "Commentary—The Disease as Cure," 147, 152.

31 480 U.S. 616, 657–77 (1987).

32 Posner, "The DeFunis Case," 16.

I   The Central Argument

1 I later argue that even if this assertion may be challenged, the Equal Protection Clause nonetheless makes most sense if based on the assumption that it is true (see pp. 24–29 in this volume).

2 Bureau of the Census, 1980 *Census of Population: General Social and Economic Characteristics; U.S. Summary*, table 80, p. I-18; *State and Metropolitan Area Data Handbook 1986*, table C: States: Movers, Marital Status and Households, 511; *Detailed Population Characteristics; U.S. Summary*, sect. A, table 259, p. I-20; *Statistical Abstract of the United States, 1987*, table 29, p. 25.

3 Of the twenty largest cities in the United States, Washington, D.C., is tied for first place in terms of disproportionate numbers of women. San Diego and San Francisco rank first and second, respectively, in having disproportionate numbers of men. See National Decision Systems, 1980 *United States Census: Population and Housing Characteristics*, PF (vol.) 1, p. 80.

4 The labels *interpretivism* and *noninterpretivism* were popularized by John Hart Ely, who characterized the former as "indicating that judges deciding constitutional issues should confine themselves to enforcing norms that are stated or clearly implicit in the written Constitution, the latter the contrary view that courts should go beyond that set of references and enforce norms that cannot be discovered within the four corners of the document" (Ely, *Democracy and Distrust: A Theory of Judicial Review* [Cambridge, Mass.: Harvard University Press, 1980], 1).

5 Unfortunately, since the amendment's passage was the result of complicated political (and ambivalent personal) calculations, it cannot be assumed that even its supporters all believed that whites and blacks are truly equal at birth.

6 *Plessy v. Ferguson*, 163 U.S. 537 (1896).

7 *DeFunis v. Odegaard*, 416 U.S. 312 (1974).

8 Posner, "The DeFunis Case," 17.

9 See, for instance, Sowell, "Weber and Bakke, and the Presuppositions of 'Affirmative Action,'" 26 *Wayne L. Rev.* 1309 (1980), for an elaboration and summary of his extensive empirical criticism of "this staggering notion [that] discrimination must be the decisive explanation of intergroup differences."

10 *Id.*, at 1314–17.

11 *Id.*, at 1323.

12 For distinctions between individual and group rights based on the distinction made here between ethnicity and race—based, that is, on the argument that ethnicity might exist in a fair, nondiscriminatory world whereas race-based cultural differences would not—see pp. 57–61 in this volume.

13 Lee, "White Couples Battle Obstacles to Adoption of Nonwhite Children," *Wall Street Journal*, 27 February 1987, 1, 10.

II The Innocent Persons Argument Examined

1 438 U.S. 275 (1978).

2 Sullivan, "Sins of Discrimination," 94, citing in particular Chief Justice Burger in *Fullilove v. Klutznick*, 448 U.S. 448, 485 (1980): "It was within congressional power to act on the assumption that in the past some nonminority businesses may have reaped competitive benefit over the years from the virtual exclusion of minority firms from [public] contracting opportunities."

3 438 U.S. 265, at 365–66 (opinion of Brennan, White, Marshall, and Blackmun, JJ.).

4 Sullivan, "Sins of Discrimination," 94, quoting from *Wygant*, 476 U.S., at 280–81 (opinion of Powell, J.).

5 See, for instance, *Johnson v. Santa Clara County*, 480 U.S. 616, 657–77 (1987) (dissenting opinion of Scalia, J.); *Local Number 93, Firefighters v. Cleveland*, 478 U.S. 501, 535–45 (1986), at 3082–87 (dissenting opinion of Rehnquist, J.); *City of Richmond v. J. A. Croson Co.*, 109 S.Ct. 706, 735–39 (concurring opinion of Scalia, J.). Chief Justice Rehnquist joined Justice Powell's opinion in *Wygant*, which claimed a Court "consensus" for the proposition that the rights of innocent persons may be abridged in some cases, but it is misleading to read too much into that. The new Chief Justice's overall record indicates that he did so only because he is willing to uphold giving "constructive seniority"—the seniority that would have existed in the absence of discrimination—to known victims of an employer's discrimination, even though the white workers to be passed over are "innocent." See *Franks v. Bowman Transportation Co.*, 424 U.S. 747 (1975). But because those cases are always brought by and always focus on minority (or female) individuals who claim specific discrimination against them, such cases are not true affirmative action cases but rather straightforward discrimination cases. The fact thus remains that Chief Justice Rehnquist has never approved of sacrificing the rights of so-called innocent persons in an affirmative action case.

6 430 U.S. 144, at 174 (1977).

7 438 U.S. 265, 361–62 (1978) (opinion of Brennan, J.).

8 424 U.S. 747 (1975).

9 438 U.S. 265, 365 (1978).

10 *United Steelworkers v. Weber*, 443 U.S. 193 (1979).

11 *Johnson v. Santa Clara County*, 480 U.S. 616 (1987).

12 *Id.*, at 657 (dissenting opinion of White, J.).

13 *Local Number 93, Firefighters v. Cleveland*, 478 U.S. 501, 534, 535 (dissenting opinion of White, J.); see also *Sheet Metal Workers v. EEOC*, 478 U.S. 421, 499–500 (1986) (dissenting opinion of White, J.); *Wygant v. Jackson Board of Education*, 476 U.S. 267 (1986); *Johnson v. Santa Clara County*, 480 U.S. 616, 657 (1987) (dissenting opinion of White, J.).

14 *Sheet Metal Workers v. EEOC*, 478 U.S. 421, 494 (1986).

15 *City of Richmond v. J. A. Croson Co.*, 109 S.Ct., at 724 (1989).

16 See *Sheet Metal Workers v. EEOC*, 478 U.S. 421, 489–99 (1986) (opinion of O'Connor, J.).

17 In the most recent case, her characterization of the program in question as exhibiting goals applied flexibly in the short run rather than rigid quotas issued for an extended period was sharply challenged by Justice Scalia. See *Johnson v. Santa Clara County*, 480 U.S. 616, 653–56, 661–63 (1987) (opinions of O'Connor, J., and Scalia, J., respectively).

18 See, e.g., *Wygant v. Jackson Board of Education*, 476 U.S. 267, 282–83 (1986) (opinion of Powell, J.); *United States v. Paradise*, 480 U.S. 149, 188–89 (1987) (opinion of Powell, J.).

19 *Fullilove v. Klutznick*, 448 U.S. 448, 507 n. 7 (1980) (concurring opinion of Powell, J.).

20 *United States v. Paradise*, 480 U.S., at 189 (1987) (opinion of Powell, J.).

21 See *Johnson v. Santa Clara County*, 480 U.S. 616, 643 (1987) (concurring opinion of Stevens, J.), quoting from his opinion in *Bakke*: Congress intended "to eliminate all practices which operate to disadvantage the employment opportunities of any group protected by Title VII including Caucasians."

22 *Id.*, at 643, 644 (1987).

23 *City of Richmond v. J. A. Croson Co.*, 109 S.Ct. 706, 733 (1989) (concurring opinion of Stevens, J.).

24 *Id.*, at 734–35 (concurring opinion of Kennedy, J.).

25 Sullivan, "Sins of Discrimination," at 91–92.

26 Sher made essentially this same point: "The crucial fact about these individuals is not that they are more *responsible* for past discrimination than others . . . but rather that unless reverse discrimination is practiced they will *benefit* more [than they should]" ("Justifying Reverse Discrimination," at 164).

27 *Fullilove v. Klutznick*, 448 U.S., at 530, n. 12 (1980) (Stewart, J., dissenting), quoted in Brief for the United States as Amicus Curiae Supporting Petitioners, at 27, *Wygant* (no. 84-1340).

28 See Brief for the United States as Amicus Curiae Supporting Petitioners, at 9–11, 13, 15–17, 23–29, *Stotts* (no. 82-206).

29 See Brief for the United States as Amicus Curiae Supporting Petitioners, at 6, 26, 27, 28–29, *Wygant* (no. 84-1340); Brief for the United States as Amicus Curiae Supporting Petitioners, at 4, 6, 8, 15, 16, 23, 29, *Firefighters* (no. 84-1999); Brief for the Equal Employment Opportunity Commission, at 10–11, 12, 23, 27, 29, 33, 36, *Sheet Metal Workers* (no. 84-1656).

30 See Brief for the United States, at 15, 16, *Paradise* (no. 85-999).

31 *Sheet Metal Workers v. EEOC*, 478 U.S., at 475–76 (1986); *Local Number 93, Firefighters v.*

Cleveland, 478 U.S., at 517. The three dissenters on this question were Chief Justice Burger and Justices Rehnquist and White.

32 Solicitor General Charles Fried's reaction to the *Sheet Metal Workers* and *Firefighters* decisions was: "We have said that race-conscious remedies which are not victim-specific are never permissible. The Court has said: 'Not never, but hardly ever.'" *New York Times*, 3 July 1986, at B9, col. I.

33 *Johnson v. Santa Clara County*, 480 U.S. 616, 640–41 (1987).

34 Sher, "Justifying Reverse Discrimination," at 169–70.

III Proportionate and Disproportionate Quotas: The Key Distinction

1 Although Sher suggested the central argument here, his brief but incisive essay lacks the key distinction of proportionality. Because he did not employ the crucial device of nonracist assumptions and original positions, his position lacks a principle for distinguishing truly equitable affirmative action programs from those which arguably do still violate the rights of white males. The principle may be implicit in the author's formulation of the problem: "the key to an adequate justification of reverse discrimination [is] to see [it] not as the redressing of past privations, but rather as a way of neutralizing the present competitive disadvantage caused by those past privations and thus as a way of restoring equal access to those goods which society distributes competitively" ("Justifying Reverse Discrimination," at 163). It is not clear whether Sher believes that proportionality is the measure of both "the present competitive disadvantage" and "equal access."

2 Posner, "The *DeFunis* Case," 25.

3 Kaplan, "Equal Justice in an Unequal World," 363.

4 Posner, "The *DeFunis* Case," 25: "Would *that* go too far? Why?"

5 304 U.S. 144 (1938).

6 Dworkin, "Why Bakke Has No Case," 24 *New York Review of Books* no. 18 (10 November 1977), 12.

7 Dworkin, "A Reply by Ronald Dworkin," in *Ronald Dworkin and Contemporary Jurisprudence*, ed. Marshall Cohen (Totowa, N.J.: Rowman & Allanheld, 1984), 291.

8 See Dworkin, "Reverse Discrimination," in *Taking Rights Seriously* (Cambridge, Mass.: Harvard University Press, 1977), esp. at 227–29; Dworkin, "What Is Equality," parts 1 and 2, 10 *Philosophy and Public Affairs* nos. 3 and 4 (Summer and Fall 1981).

9 438 U.S. 265, at 374, n. 58 (opinion of Brennan, White, Marshall, and Blackmun, JJ.).

10 *Id.*

11 *Id.*

12 *Id.*, at 404 (opinion of Blackmun, J., concurring).

13 478 U.S. 421 (1986).

14 *Id.*, at 487 (concurring opinion of Powell, J.).

15 448 U.S. 448, at 510–11 (1980).

16 480 U.S. 149, 199 (1987).

17 Justice O'Connor's *Paradise* dissent was joined by Chief Justice Rehnquist and Justice Scalia.

18 480 U.S., at 197 (O'Connor, J., dissenting); citations omitted.

19 Perhaps the best evidence that the Court has not accepted the proportionality argument is one of its most recent decisions. In *United States v. Paradise*, 480 U.S. 149 (1987), the Court upheld a disproportionate quota, albeit under extreme circumstances and where the quota was employed more as a threat than a fact.

20 Sullivan, "Sins of Discrimination," 78.

21 *United States v. Paradise*, 480 U.S. 149 (1987).

22 Brief for the United States, *United States v. Paradise*, no. 85-999, October Term, 1986, at 17–18; citations omitted.

23 *Regents v. Bakke*, 438 U.S., at 291 (opinion of Powell, J.). The *Wygant* plurality had also cited this fact as evidence that Justice White agreed with their position.

24 448 U.S. 448, 551 (1980) (Stevens, J., dissenting).

25 Brief for the United States, *United States v. Paradise*, no. 85-999, October Term, 1986, at 18, n. 7.

26 388 U.S. 1 (1967).

27 Id., at 9.

28 *McLaughlin v. Florida*, 379 U.S. 184, 192 (1964).

29 388 U.S., at 10–11.

30 See also *McLaughlin v. Florida*, 379 U.S. 184 (1964), in which the Court invalidated a statute making interracial cohabitation a crime and imposing a greater penalty than for cohabitation between those of the same race.

31 See, *e.g.*, 110 *Congressional Record* 6549 (1964); id., at 6566; id., at 14665. This statutory reading is essentially shared by Fallon and Weiler, "*Firefighters v. Stotts*," 14–15 and notes.

32 "Nothing contained in this title shall be interpreted to require any employer . . . to grant preferential treatment to any individual . . . because of [his/her] race . . . on account of an imbalance which may exist with respect to the total number or percentage of persons of any race . . . employed . . . in comparison with the total number or percentage of persons of such race . . . in any community, State, section, or other area, or in the available work force in any community, State, section or other areas." See *United Steelworkers v. Weber*, 443 U.S. 193, 205, n. 5 (1979).

33 Fallon and Weiler, 24; emphasis added.

34 See *Sheet Metal Workers v. EEOC*, 478 U.S. 421, 463–65 (1986) (opinion of Brennan, J.); at 490–99 (opinion of O'Connor, J.).

35 Sullivan, "Sins of Discrimination," 80; citations omitted.

36 Id., at 98.

37 At a later point Sullivan referred to "the *perception* of innocence that the paradigm of sin *sets up*," and argued that "[t]he problem with sin as the predicate for affirmative action is . . . that it *keeps alive* protests about windfalls to nonvictims and injustice to innocents" (id., at 95–96; emphasis added). Her repeated use of quotation marks around the word *innocence* makes the same point: the innocence is only apparent, not real.

38 Id., at 80.

39 Id., at 96.

40 Although it may be unfair to read so much into these brief comments, Sullivan's suggestion appears to be compatible with, if not identical to, the assumptions of a

compensatory justice defense of affirmative action. As such, it is vulnerable to the common and very serious objections to that approach.

41 Sullivan, "Sins of Discrimination," at 80.

42 *Id.*

43 *Id.*, at 96.

44 Dworkin, "Reverse Discrimination"; Dworkin, "Why Bakke Has No Case"; also see Dworkin, "The Bakke Case: An Exchange" [hereinafter: "Exchange"], 24 *New York Review of Books* no. 18 (10 November 1977), 11–15, nos. 21 and 22 (26 January 1978), 42–44, respectively.

45 Dworkin, "Why Bakke Has No Case," at 11.

46 *Id.*, at 12.

47 *Id.*, at 11.

48 *Id.*, at 15.

49 *Id.*

50 *Id.*, at 13.

51 Dworkin, "Exchange," 44.

52 Dworkin's rebuttal of critics of his piece on Bakke began with the observation that the "many letters to the [*New York Review of Books*], only a few of which could be published, confirm that Bakke's supporters are largely people of very good will who hate racial prejudice but who are deeply worried about either the fairness or the wisdom of affirmative action" ("Exchange," at 44).

53 This characterization of Dworkin's position is John Robertson's, in a "Letter to the Editors," in "Exchange."

54 *Id.*

55 "Reverse Discrimination," 228.

56 *Id.*, 226.

57 *Id.*, at 228.

58 Sullivan, "Sins of Discrimination," 98.

IV   Applying the Principles: The Supreme Court and Affirmative Action

1 See *Baker v. Carr*, 369 U.S. 186, 217 (1962).

2 Reported in the Bucks County (Pa.) *Courier Times*, 28 June 1986, 3.

3 In employment discrimination cases there is, of course, a whole body of law regarding the appropriate area on which to base the proportion. The original case is *Hazelwood School District v. United States*, 433 U.S. 299 (1977).

4 Scalia, "Commentary—The Disease as Cure," 147, 159.

5 443 U.S. 193 (1979); 480 U.S. 149 (1987).

6 443 U.S., at 193.

7 *NAACP v. Alabama*, 340 F. Supp. 703, 705 (M.D. Ala. 1972), reprinted in *Paradise* (Jt. App.).

8 *Paradise v. Shoemaker*, 470 F. Supp. 439, 442 (M.D. Ala. 1979) (emphasis in original). See J.A. 63; Pet. App. 10a–12a.

9 J.A. 52, 53. See 29 C.F.R. 1607.4(D). Cited in Brief for United States, at 6, 7, *Paradise* (no. 85-999).

10 Pet. App. 14a; J.A. 119. Cited *id.*, at 7.

11 Pet. App. 14a–15a. The characterization is the United States's own. Brief for United States, at 8, *Paradise* (no. 85-999).

12 Pet. App. 15a; J.A. 60.

13 Pet. App. 15a; J.A. 58–62.

14 J.A. 123, quoted in Brief for the United States, at 10–11, *Paradise* (no. 85-999).

15 J.A. 128, 129.

16 Brief for the United States at 16, *Paradise* (no. 85-999).

17 *Id.*

18 *Id.*, at 17.

19 467 U.S. 561 (1984); 476 U.S. 265 (1986).

20 The quota was part of a collective bargaining agreement between the board of education and the teachers' association of Jackson, Michigan. It stated that "at no time will there be a greater percentage of minority personnel laid off than the current percentage of minority personnel employed at the time of the layoff" (Pet. App. 3a). Although the agreement also stated that the goal of the layoff provision was "to have at least the same percentage of minority racial representation on each individual staff as is represented by the student population of the Jackson Public Schools" (*id.*, at 13a, 22a, 32a), nowhere in the briefs submitted to the Supreme Court is either the actual teacher ratio or the actual student ratio specified. The fact that the Court treated these omissions as inconsequential is, of course, further evidence of its indifference to the proportionality argument.

21 The characterization is from one of the city's defenders. Brief for the United States as Amicus Curiae in Support of Petitioners, nos. 82-206, 82-229, n. 3, at 3.

22 Brief for the United States as Amicus Curiae in Support of Petitioners, nos. 82-206, 82-229, at 2–3.

23 *Id.*, n. 3, at 3.

24 These figures are available in the administration's *amicus* brief, *id.*, at 4 and n. 6, although they are couched in terms that disguise the dramatic disproportionate effect the layoff proposal would have had.

25 42 U.S.C. (& Supp. V) 2000e *et seq.*

26 Brief for the United States as Amicus Curiae in Support of Petitioners, nos. 82-206, 82-229, at 18; emphasis added.

27 *Id.* The case cited is *Ford Motor Co. v. EEOC*, 458 U.S. 219, 240 (1982). The administration also cited *Arizona Governing Committee v. Norris*, 463 U.S. 1073, 1110 (1983) (O'Connor, J., concurring).

28 Brief for the United States, at 18. The cited passage is from *Teamsters v. United States*, 431 U.S. 324, 372 (1977).

29 Brief for the United States, at 21–22.

30 467 U.S. 561, at 575.

31 *Id.*, at 579, n. 11.

32 *Id.*, at 620–21 (opinion of Blackmun, J., dissenting).

33 Sher, "Justifying Reverse Discrimination," 164, n. 7.

34 *Id.*

Epilogue

1 See Cohen, "At Georgetown: Taboos," *Washington Post*, 26 April 1991, A23: "'diversity' . . . is the term of the moment for affirmative action."

2 Steele, "A Negative Vote on Affirmative Action," *New York Times Magazine*, 13 May 1990, 46ff.

3 See Wycliff, "Blacks Debate the Costs of Affirmative Action," *New York Times*, 10 June 1990, 3.

4 *Albany Times-Union*, 19 May 1991, B1.

5 See Liebman, "Implementing Brown in the Nineties: Political Reconstruction, Liberal Recollection, and Litigatively Enforced Legislative Reform," 76 *Virginia L. Rev.* 349 (1990), and Liebman, "Desegregating Politics: 'All-Out' School Desegregation Explained," 90 *Columbia L. Rev.* 1463 (1990).

6 Liebman, "Desegregating Politics," 1598–99.

7 Liebman, "Implementing Brown," 363.

8 See Liebman, "Desegregating Politics," 1600.

9 110 S.Ct. 2997 (1990).

10 Id., at 3008–9.

11 Id., at 3011.

12 Id.

13 Id., at 3022, 3012.

14 Id., at 3024.

15 Id., at 3027.

16 Id., at 3029.

17 Id., at 3034.

18 Id.

19 Id., at 3031.

20 Id., at 3032.

21 See id., at 3037, 3038.

22 See id., at 3039.

23 Id., at 3046.

24 Id., at 3047.

25 109 S.Ct. 706.

26 109 S.Ct. 2115 (1989).

27 109 S.Ct. 2180 (1989).

28 109 S.Ct. 2261 (1989).

29 109 S.Ct. 2383 (1989).

30 427 U.S. 160 (1976).

31 109 S.Ct. 1775 (1989).

32 109 S.Ct. 2732 (1989). In addition, also not helpful to the cause of reducing discrimination in employment was the ruling in *Jett v. Dallas Independent School District*, 109 S.Ct. 2702 (1989), that when there was employment discrimination in violation of 42 U.S.C. § 1981, a municipality could not be sued under that statute for the behavior of its employees on a theory of *respondeat superior*. See also *Will v. Michigan Department of State Police*, 109 S.Ct. 2304 (1989), another employment case, in which

the majority ruled that neither a state nor officials in their official capacity were "persons" for purpose of the civil rights statute (sec. 1983).

33 See, for example, Greenberg and Lee, "For Affirmative Action, Richmond Decision Is a Detour, Not a Dead End," *Los Angeles Times*, 8 February 1990, II, 13.

34 401 U.S. 424 (1971).

35 For a useful discussion of this point and the "quota" problem, see Williams and Allen, "Candid Talk about Quotas," *Washington Post*, 9 December 1990, K1, K4.

36 See Holmes, "Adjusting of Test Scores Inflames Rights Debate," *New York Times*, 17 May 1990, A12; Kilborn, " 'Race Norming' Tests Becomes a Fiery Issue," *New York Times*, 19 May 1991, 16; and, for an example of a conservative opinion leader's opposition, see Will, "Do Away with Race-Norming," *The Capital* (Annapolis), 26 May 1991, A10.

37 See Lewis, "Race and College Aid," *New York Times*, 13 December 1990, B15.

38 DeBenedictis, "Minority Recruitment Warning," 77 *ABA Journal* 14–15 (January 1991).

39 Rosenthal, "White House in Disarray," *New York Times*, 20 December 1990, 1, B18.

table of cases

index

146 : Index

150 : Index

U.S. Commission on Civil Rights, 124

Victims, 5, 44–48, 82. *See also* "Innocent persons" argument
Voting rights, xii–xiii, 53; Republicans, 125–26. *See also* Voting Rights Act
Voting Rights Act of 1965, xii–xiii, 126; 1982 amendments, 122

Warren, Earl, 67
Washington, D.C., 22–23, 133 n.3
Weiler, Paul C., 11, 70–71, 130–31 n.7, 133 n.29, 137 nn.31 and 33
White, Byron, 41–42, 61, 66, 107, 116,

130 n.3, 132 n.17, 135 nn.12 and 13, 136 n.9
White-collar jobs, 78, 90–91
White males, 4–5, 11, 13–14, 64, 82, 121, 136 n.1. *See also* "Innocent persons" argument
Whites, 10, 13, 39, 42, 44, 46, 49–52, 91, 94, 96–100, 102–12; difference from blacks, 15–17, 19–21, 23–29, 32–37, 69, 77, 120. *See also* Innocent persons
Williams, Michael L., 124–25
Women: different from men, 15–16, 22–23, 133 n.3. *See also* Gender discrimination

About the Author. Ronald J. Fiscus was Assistant Professor of
Political Science at Skidmore College at the time of his death in
1990. He received his Ph.D. from the University of Wisconsin,
Madison, in 1982.

    About the Editor. Stephen L. Wasby is Professor of Political
Science at the State University of New York at Albany. His
writing focuses on civil rights and the federal courts. His many
books include *The Supreme Court in the Federal Judicial System, Vote
Dilution: Minority Voting Rights and the Courts,* and *"He Shall Not Pass
This Way Again": The Legacy of Justice William O. Douglas.*

Library of Congress Cataloging-in-Publication Data
Fiscus, Ronald Jerry.
The constitutional logic of affirmative action / Ronald J. Fiscus :
edited by Stephen L. Wasby.
Includes bibliographical references and index.
ISBN 0-8223-1206-9 (cloth : alk. paper)
  1. Affirmative action programs—Law and legislation—United
States—Philosophy. 2. Distributive justice. I. Wasby, Stephen
L., 1937– . II. Title.
KF4755.5.F57   1992
342.73'0873—dc20
[347.302873] 91-33695 CIP